# Do you have a story? Please share it with us!

Golden Fleece Press is always open for submissions. Check out our website for more information about submissions and upcoming projects. We also have a mailing list!

Check us out at goldenfleecepress.com

Print ISBN 978-1-942195-34-4

PDF ISBN 978-1-942195-35-1

Edited by Ashley K. Voris

# A Long Time Ago
# On A Couch
# On A Sidewalk

## Christina Gleeson

I wasn't really a big Star Wars fan when I was a kid. I'd watched the movies, of course, but I hadn't been bitten by the fandom bug. Why, then, did I find myself sleeping on a couch on the sidewalk in order to get Star Wars movie tickets?

The answer, in short, was love. Tom was my boyfriend at the time, but he is my husband now. We celebrated our 15th anniversary the same week tickets went on sale for *The Force Awakens*. But this story is really about *The Phantom Menace*, back in a time where Jar-Jar Binks wasn't a punchline, and Star Wars fans were just really, really excited to finally get the prequel trilogy they'd been waiting for.

In his college days, Tom lived in his fraternity house. The less said about that dirty, disgusting house, the better. He and his fraternity brothers happened to share a love of Star Wars, so when tickets were going to be available for sale at the box office, they made plans. Yes, this was a time in which Fandango did not exist, nor did smartphones. People had to physically transport themselves to the point of sale and exchange cash (or an actual plastic credit card) for paper movie tickets.

Because of the hype surrounding Episode I's release, Tom and his brothers wanted to ensure they could get into the midnight showing at the nearest movie theater to be among the first to bear witness to this historic event. And I, being a dutiful girlfriend who was either already home for the summer or had snuck home for the weekend, came along for the festivities.

We arrived at the front of the Madison Theater when it was still daylight the day before tickets went on sale. We were not the first crazy people to show up that early; there were several devoted young men who had arrived even earlier.

This theater was not inside a mall; it was a standalone building on a city block, and we would be waiting on the sidewalk overnight.

I don't know when the decision was made or who suggested it, but the fraternity decided it would be far better to wait it out if we could do so in comfort. I stayed behind as one of those who held our place in line. Time passed, but surely enough, the boys returned with a frat house sofa tied onto the roof of a car. The sofa was lifted down off the car and set where "our spot" was in line.

As the token female of the group, I got priority when it came to claiming a spot on the couch. I slept, though others stayed awake all night. We got our tickets the next day, and I went with the rowdy bunch to watch the first showing of Episode I: *The Phantom Menace*, taking in all of the fans who had come in costume.

I wouldn't sleep on a couch for movie tickets ever again, but it will make a fun story to tell when we have grand kids. For the record, I don't care if Han shot first; I actually prefer the prequel trilogy to the original trilogy. Tom and I will continue to agree to disagree about this for the rest of our lives.

# If My Mother Had Lived: A Poem by Luke Skywalker

Melissa Crayton

If mother had lived, life would've been grand.

Living on a lush green planet, instead of a world made of sand

If mom had lived, I could've been great,

Instead of twiddling my thumbs on a planet I hate.

I could've gone to great schools and learned all about politics.

I might've been king of Naboo by the time I was six.

I wouldn't have tried to kiss my twin that time on Endor

She is such a babe but I can't think like that anymore.

A pet Voorpak would have beat old womprats for fun

And oh to live on a planet with only one sun

Vacationing on the lakes would've been a dream

Instead of living on the dusty old cesspool, Tatooine.


Maybe Jar Jar Binks would've babysat us while on Naboo

Maybe we would've had weekend visits with Vader to look forward to

Of course the rumor is that Binks is a Sith, like old Dad

But I reckon even the dark side isn't entirely bad.

In the end he showed a little goodness, I guess

But having Mom my whole life would've been best

Maybe she would've had more kids and I would've had a half-brother

But we will never know now since my dad choked my mother.

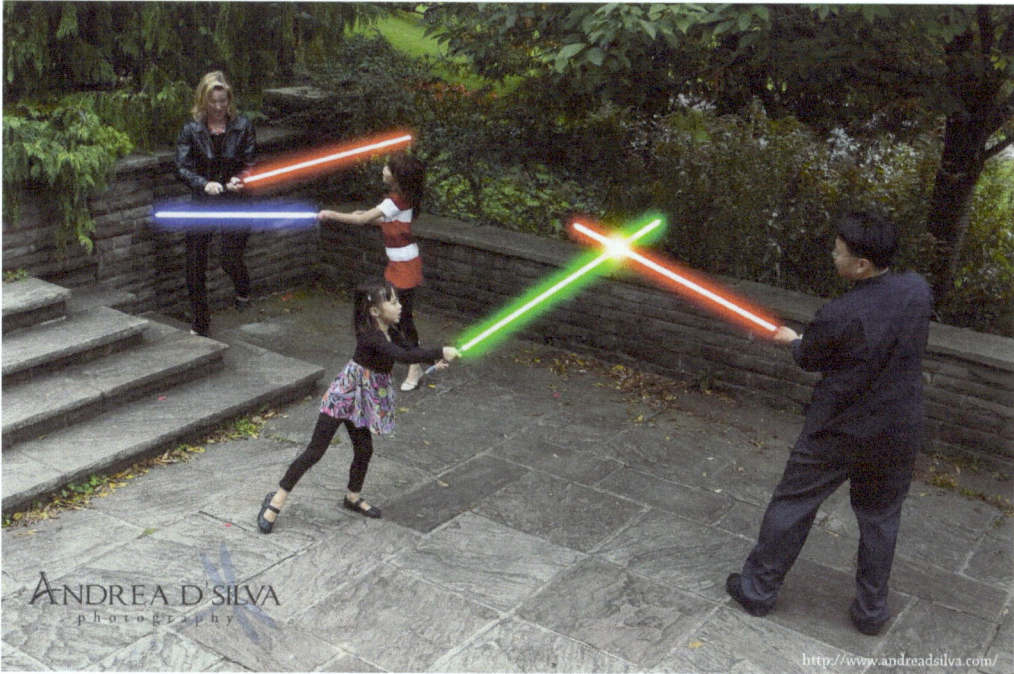

# The Force is strong in this family. Geek parenting at its finest.

Check out Andrea D'Silva's awesome photgraphy at andreadsilva.com

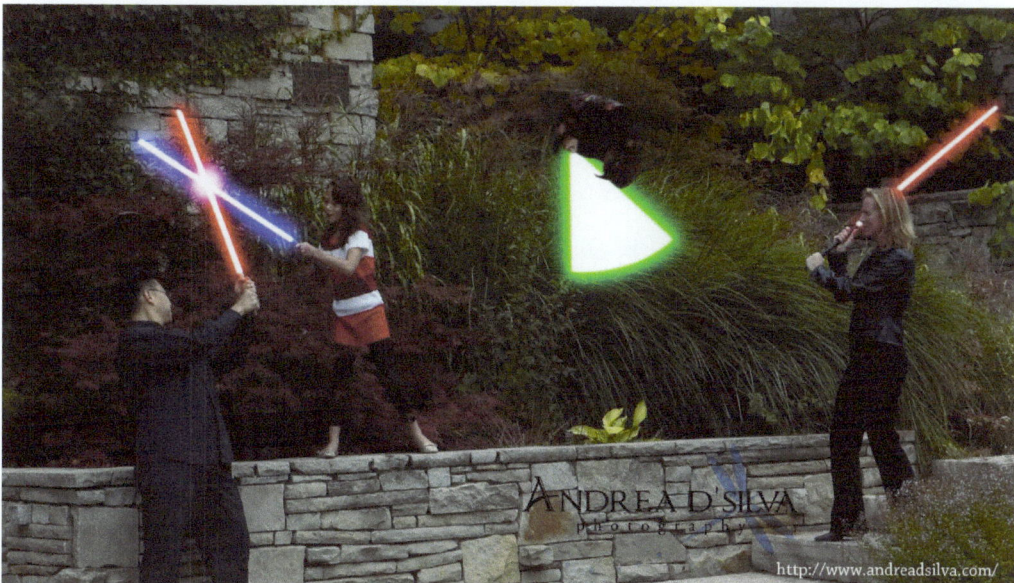

# Darth Solo

## Jason Gaff

I have not always worked or played well with others which I credit to a decided preference for playing on my own that began when I was a kid. This wasn't the case at all times, though, one could hardly solo at football, soccer, baseball or any of the other sport-hybrids I and the other athletic conceptualists of Chapel Valley invented. My old neighbors might tell a different story of the odd boy next door tossing a football down field then running after it; a situation I only found myself in when needing to scratch a competitive itch so badly that there was no time to call up some chums, get teams organized and so on. The crude video games made for my Atari also required another player in order for it to seem fun. I was never a good enough gamer to go it alone.

When left to play in the imaginative galaxy of my Kenner Star Wars toys, however, was when my preference for solitude was strongest. Other kids just screwed things up. If you had a cool toy like the Imperial Armored Transport which was the size of a small dog and had been featured in *The Empire Strikes Back* to convey the Empire's stormtroopers across the icy surface of the planet Hoth, I'd probably come over to your house to play with you. Understand that in such cases my interest was concentrated on the toy rather than on any hackneyed scenario you wanted us to act out together. I'd much rather play on my own and develop ideas that seemed to only upset so many of my compatriots. Chief among them was an endgame in which Darth Vader reigned victorious in the final, inevitable showdown with Luke Skywalker.

Vader was both terrifying and enthralling, ruling a not so small piece of my childhood from the ages of about four to eleven years old. I don't think I was alone in my admiration for the Emperor's second in command, the Dark Lord. It was a passion, like all those that burn the most fervently at that age, which had to be kept from the outside world. Even secretly advocating for Vader triumphing, did set me apart from my playmates and prepared me well for the long years of isolation and loneliness that were to follow.

When the prequels to the three original *Star Wars* films were released, they made it abundantly clear that creator George Lucas had always intended *Star Wars* to be Darth Vader's nee Anakin Skywalker's story. The whole shooting match went something like this: as a callow young Jedi in training, Anakin goes astray, fights his mentor, loses, gets burnt to a crisp, becomes the head of the Republican Party before revealing he's been Humpty Dumpty all along. Nothing but plain old pipe tobacco as far as narratives go, the rise and fall followed by redemption dance. It's the basic ingredients needed for turning a regular tale into an epic one. A hero rises through hard work under the tutelage of a caring mentor, soon he wants to know and do more than the mentor thinks appropriate. The hero soon unduly constrained, turns against his mentor and becomes a bad boy who kills his old tutor only later to repent and finally, through the love of either a lost child or a woman finds the strength to forgive himself and go on thereby spiritually reuniting with the mentor, who had preached forgiveness and love all along.

The very same scenario played out on a season long story arc on *The Facts of Life*. Who can forget the penultimate episode that ended with Blair remorsefully standing over Mrs. Garret's blood-stained corpse? The way the old gal's coarse, red wig drooped from her skull into a slowly gathering pool of blood suggested all we thought we knew of the world was wrong. Blair had gone from the show's popular glamour girl to one who'd always be haunted by her past, doomed to roam the Earth in a fog of loneliness and unmitigated remorse. Such is the curse of the soul doomed by her own actions to a life of solitude.

At Darth's local, he's surely got his own stool at the far end in the corner. No friends to speak of but acquaintances aplenty, drinking buddies. A stormtrooper that once guarded him might show up to pay tribute.

# Darth Solo (cont)

'Hey, Barkeep. 'Ow bout a coupla frosty ones for me and the Dark Lord here?' Maybe Jabba the Hutt will show up later and they'll split some chicken wings. And while it's as jovial as it can be when one is sharing a meal with a slob who has to take that last wing even though he's already had more than his share, Darth mostly dreams of the moment when Jabba leaves and he can be alone again. The cruel, empty-headed automatons that work for the Empire will never understand love the way Vader does. He's given everything, including his own humanity, for it. It must be hard to listen to some white-armored shithead blabber on and on about Hoth and how much fun they had smashing up the rebel base there when all you want to do is wallow in your dead Padme's love, now lost with her, never to return.

Darth doesn't drink to meet new people either, which is a shame because that's why they call them pubs, short for public houses. It's the best place to get to know one's neighbors. Put your time in at the bar and you'll soon have more friends than you know what to do with. They'll seek you out when they come in, get you to say something clever and little by Stuart Littlish get you to forget the night is even happening.

Any kind of mourning for lost loves including post-divorce drinking is best done this way. You form attachments with others because you go through it together, swimming all the way to the bottom until you get drunk often and deeply enough to find the courage to resurface.

Essentially, Anakin was a loner by nature so his path through life was always going to be a search for solitude that tragically leads to isolation. People do get too good at asking for what they want. He fell in love with Padme, then failed to save her even though he'd turned to the dark side of the Force specifically for that reason, that and those Sith know how to make a cup of coffee, it's just so watery and thin over at the Jedi confabs.

Long before all of the action unfolded on the screen, Vader had decided to go it alone. I'd argue it was inside of him at birth. Sure he's tormented by Padme's death but there's also an air of: 'Sorry Princess, I'm just not ready to be a dad right now.' Sad, sad, sad, I know but how many men in his position would've done the same thing? Before you answer, remember it is best to lie to oneself only when you have to. The hissy fit he throws much later in the form of his failed duel with his mentor, Obi Wan was all for show. Anakin just wanted some time to himself. How many of the Siths have a different variation of that same story to tell? Darth's just happens to be the one we know.

And do not underestimate how far into a bad mood being burnt the freak up on over 90% of your body will put you. Before you all geek out on me, I'm not sure what the exact extent of Anakin's injuries were. I didn't do up some fake forensics report on it like some virgin who still lives in his mom's basement. It's a guesstimate. Anyway, the Emperor saves him and Vader gets put into his new robotic body. And since his nerve endings have all been singed off he not only feels like a robot but he also *feels* like a robot. What kind of state of mind does that put one in? Well, I've never once heard a cyborg say that getting all banged up to the point that their body had to be replaced by a machine was the best thing that ever happened to them. RoboCop would've given his left nut to go back to being just Cop, if he still had one that is.

I wore braces and can attest that they turn one a bit sullen. You don't want to smile because no matter what you mother says it's a total horror show when you do, a mouth more machine than man. And I might not have gone through getting all extra crispy but those things hurt like heck when Dr. T was done getting them all tight. I could barely chew for days afterwards. I think it's part of the reason I eat so fast now. 'Alright, teeth, let's get this sub sandwich over with.'

So did braces select me or did I choose to have bad teeth? Who can say? It may have been another case of the man choosing the path that choseth the man. Even after I was done with the braces, I had to wear this thing called a Frankle. It fit snugly in my mouth and I wore it dutifully. Its purpose was to make my mouth larger. I was born with a small mouth and it's been a lifelong goal to make it wider. And yet, I actually say very little. Speak a lot though. Maybe cheering for Vader just came as naturally.

Only a true solitarian would root for one of the most fearsome villains ever committed to film. Not Dracula, not the Wolfman, not any of the characters

# Darth Solo (cont)

Pauly Shore ever played, indeed not even Pauly himself can measure up to Vader. None of the characters in *Encino Man* were put in a choke hold by 'The Weasel' simply bringing his thumb and forefinger closer and closer together. I was savvy enough not to cheer for Vader out loud, mind you. Solitude and excommunication are two completely different things. One represents the isolation that each choice we make brings us closer to, incrementally, the other is to be first hunted, then despised then cast outside the city gates and never permitted to reenter; a little like the ending to *Biodome*.

No, one does not hoot and holler as Vader blasts his way onto some Rebel smuggling vessel. If it was a consular ship where was the goddamn ambassador? One would be excluded from any Star Wars related activity for life. Wanting to play alone and having to are two completely different ideas. Me running under a pass that I also threw was because no one else was around. Me seeing to it that the empire crushes the rebellion with Vader convincing Luke to turn to the dark side had to be done alone, no matter how much sense it made. If you face things from the darkness with the light behind you, you'll see them better.

Plus:

'Luke,' two heavy breaths, 'isn't Vader just a better last name,' four heavy breaths, 'Skywalker's pretty ridiculous,' two heavy breaths, 'sounds like a made up name for an actor in an Ewok porn,' three heavy breaths, 'not that I've watched any,' two heavy breaths, 'I mean, I may have accidentally seen a clip on Youtube,' four heavy breaths, 'Admiral Akbar sent one as a joke,' four heavy breaths, 'that guy's a real cut-up,' two heavy breaths, 'wish I could get him to join our side.'

The last of the films, *Return of the Jedi*, really seals the whole who's-trilogy-is-this deal. As a kid I thought the title was referencing Luke somehow. The crowd I ran with found him pretty annoying which is how it always is with  with this episodic epics. The main character can't be too interesting. He or she needs to be a kind of blank space on which the audience can project their hopes, dreams, the very complexity of their souls. The bland everyman and woman wants someone to carry the torch for them. In this case, first a baby blue one and then later neon green one.

'Let's face it Luke,' four heavy breaths, 'Obi Wan didn't know a thing about picking out a cool lightsaber,' two heavy breaths, 'check mine out,' sound of Vader's lightsaber blazing to life, 'no mix ups in the locker room at the Y about who this one belongs to,' two heavy breaths, sound of lightsaber cutting through the air, 'I'll take more than one towel if I want,' two heavy breaths, 'I'm, Darth Vader, damn it, I could crush your wrinkled old-man testicles like grapes with the merest blink of an eye,' two heavy breaths, 'Governor Tarkin.'

Once it was over, I realized *Return of the Jedi* was about Anakin returning to himself after his wilderness time where he had been tested by evil. It's a little like the story of the Savior in the desert and no Sixer fans, I am not talking about Barkley playing for the Suns. At the very end of that final film, when Luke, the very incubus who wrecked Padme's vajay-jay so badly that she died from blood loss, removes his dad's helmet, he allows Vader to reclaim his humanity and die as men die. Darth Vader breathes his last, he does not shut down.

At that, my black little heart broke even though I knew this was how it was supposed to end. It was Vader's story after all. Once he departed so did the impetus for the narrative, all evaporating into the space of some galaxy far, far away. It mirrors the only way each of us can understand our own demise. As we close our eyes that last time, the screen fades to black and the trilogy of our life ends and along with all of those bit characters who carried on dialogue with us. We can only hope that somewhere, someday there will be a kid playing with an action figure of us, figuring out a way to make the story go on, all on his own.

SOME QUESTIONS NEED ANSWERS.

# CODES

BRIANE PAGEL

*Curious? Briane Pagel has the answer.*
*http://goldenfleecepress.com/codes/*

Caught in a smog-storm, with a dead crew member, a disabled navigation system, and an estate full of guests. The Long Estate usually spends the season floating off the edge of The London, the Sugars and the Crusts frittering their days away in an endless string of parties and diversions while Blagger, Spinner, and the rest of the crew make sure everything runs smoothly. But now The London says they're off course, and they have to be cut loose. If they can't fix the navigation they'll slam into one of the other estates. Or The London. Or the ground.

Blagger and Spinner have only hours to find their missing equipment, solve a murder, and still keep the guests from realizing there's a problem. They can probably manage it.

As long as nothing else goes wrong.

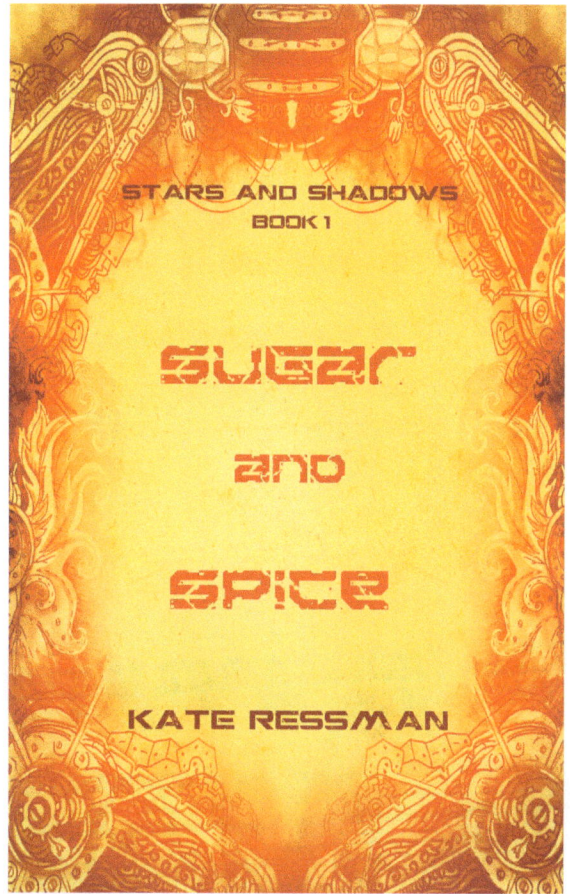

**STARS AND SHADOWS**
BOOK 1

# sugar

## and

## spice

**KATE RESSMAN**

*Available for purchase at goldenfleecepress.com*

# GOLDEN FLEECE PRESS

Need more stuff to read? Check out our ever growing catalogue. We even have a mailing list so you can be notified when a new book is released. Have a story to share? We want to hear it! Our website contains all the infomration you need to submit your query. Remember: *"There is no greater agony than bearing and untold story inside you".* (Maya Angelou)

# A FAMILY THAT STAR WARS TOGETHER STAYS TOGETHER

Been scaring her all day 😂😂🧡

# THERE IS GOOD IN YOU

## KITTY BOWERMAN

*"Fear is the path to the dark side. Fear leads to anger. Anger leads to hate. Hate leads to suffering."*

**- YODA**

As an only child, I saw my life as a constant struggle. Never mind that I had no discernible challenges or obstacles. I still feared the unknown, was easily angered, and hated school. For a young white girl living affluently in America, I convinced myself that I was endlessly suffering. Let's see, I had fear, anger, hate, suffering...

It's no wonder that I sympathized with the dark side. *The Empire Strikes Back* came out when I was six years old. It was not scary to me, in fact, I saw Darth Vader as someone to emulate (minus the violence and killing, of course). He was sharply-dressed, calm under pressure, and totally in control. And whether he was marching into the Hoth base or pacing on the bridge of a Star Destroyer, he looked good doing it.

While Vader was ultimately a tragic figure, I took the more positive messages of his storyline to help me through life. He was, after all, resilient in the face of numerous setbacks, and though villainous for the majority of Episodes IV-VI, he redeems himself at the very end. If he could endure through so much, I could certainly get through high school!

As an adult, I realized that my suffering was self-created, but continued to struggle with confidence. When it was time to get a job in the big city of Chicago, this small town girl needed to put her best face forward.

Thankfully, my favorite Jedi is a model of poise and I channeled my inner Sith for job interviews:

1. Wear a mask. Show people only what they need to see.
2. Stand tall and sit up straight (Vader does not slouch).
3. When you speak, make it memorable and meaningful. Don't talk too much.
4. A chic, all-black ensemble is the perfect uniform.

It worked! The next month, I found myself walking down Michigan Avenue in shiny black boots, black leather gloves, and a long black cashmere coat that blew majestically behind me in the wind. It was the best feeling in the world, and as I looked around me, I thought, there'll be nothing to stop me this time.

# The Mark Hamill Award
## Jaimie Vowels

Right now, in an old packed box in my apartment, sits a beautiful plaque that I was awarded a decade ago. The Mark Hamill Award is given to seniors at my high school—the same high school the actor Mark Hamill attended. I should be proud of the plaque, but I have other things that hang on my wall instead. This plaque is given to students who succeed in both academics and performing arts. I am very proud of the fact I was able to earn this award. With the prequel trilogy coming out at that time, *Star Wars* had nearly as much attention as it does now. However, I quickly realized that after I graduated and mentioned this award, I was met by blank stares. The most common response I received was "Who's that?" I would then have to explain that he was the guy who played Luke Skywalker, one of the stars in *Star Wars*. I would just get a nod or a shrug. It is like people forget who he is or they don't care.

The truth is, Mark Hamill has an amazing legacy. Beyond Star Wars, he has a long standing career as the voice of The Joker across many mediums, and has done an amazing job. He has remained successful throughout this career and I think he will only go forward. But his absence of thought about Mark Hamill is driven home by the new trailers and posters for *Star Wars: The Force Awakens*. Why is this star forgotten, like my shiny plaque at home? Why is Mark Hamill always cast in the shadow of Star Wars? When will he truly get to shine?

"This war will never end as long as both sides have time machines," Barbara warned, "because one side will always be able to travel back and checkmate the other."

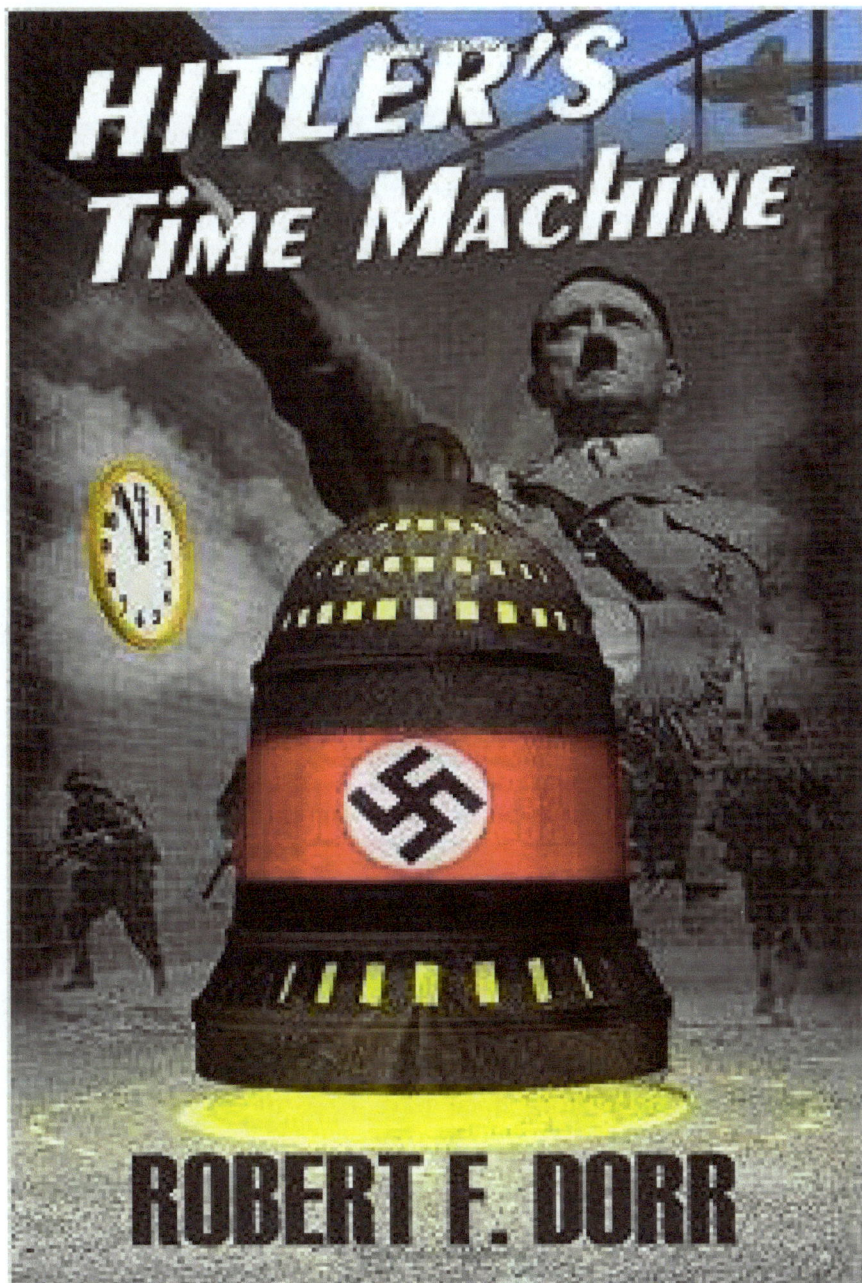

Robert F. Dorr is an author and retired senior American diplomat who has authored 70 books and numerous articles on international affairs, military issues and the Vietnam War.

# Reading Star Wars
## Jessica Engel

I used to stay up nights reading different *Star Wars* books. I originally got invested in the Young Jedi Knights books. Loved seeing Jaina Solo and Jacen Solo grow up and face the dark reality of some of the galaxy while still keeping an innocent youth about them, hoping for the good in people. And as they were tested they learned a lot about themselves.

The relationship between Jacen Solo and Tenel Ka, from the first moments and his awkward jokes to book 4: *Lightsabers* with testing out their lightsabers in a duel that ended in the tragic loss of her arm. But how she still moved on with her life and didn't let it end their friendship. After they grew up and the characters were taken by other authors for other books, the joy of that camaraderie was lost. And I think it wasn't just them being older, it was a different view, and they were really used more as plot points.

Maybe though, it was just difficult seeing children making more adult-like mistakes. They were also being treated as adults, and judged that way too. The way Kevin J. Anderson and Rebecca Moesta wrote the children they always had a safety net of adults watching them even when they went off on their own and difficult and dangerous events ensued.

I read other books outside that series, too. *Children of the Jedi* is still stuck in my head. Half of the book was on Luke trapped in the ship called Eye of Palpatine and him connecting with the entity of the ship's computer, a spirit that was a female Jedi Knight. I must have been listening to one Kenny G album when reading this book. I still listen to it so when the song "The Moment" comes on I'm transported to sitting on my twin bed, stuffed animals lining the railing. I'm reading this book with the fights, the struggle in the hazy pain-filled dreaming having to wake up and break out with unexpected help. And I always think of the failed love story that became of Callista and Luke in later books, part of the problem being that she had taken over another woman's body towards the end of this book and couldn't accept her new identity or the loss of powers with the Force.

It's hard to place how the books influenced my life, though I will say they taught me how to really try and take someone's descriptions of a world I could never see for myself, and try to be in that place. Not every book had good descriptions, sometimes it was always a struggle to picture an alien creature's face, but I could always hear their voices, when they were written in English anyways, instead of incomprehensible noises.

I liked being able to see how war broke out in a different setting: similar problems, but disguised from the way people in our own world create destruction and grief. But even hidden behind limbs that came out of nowhere and a culture almost nonsensical, you could always see the characters were people, with their own goals and motivations whether for more power or recognition, or just to survive and take care of the people and planets they loved.

It always made my view of the world just a little bit bigger by comparing it to the large scale, but still small challenges of the characters in each book. Also so neat to see different authors pick up the same story and go for it, still trying to find their own niche in the larger world. There was a part of me that one day wanted to add my little bit of whimsy and figure out a storyline out there. Reading those books might not have been the only ones that told me I wanted to write, but they did show me how big the world I build could be, how important each piece.

The stories became a bit of my makeup as I grew older. I learned more descriptive words, and I also started to note the differences between writing styles, easier when it's the same story world, but different writers. And I got a sense of who as writers I was most invested in reading. A bit of anger will always be there for R. A. Salvatore for killing Chewbacca in *Vector Prime*. My younger sister refused to read anymore after she was spoiled on that incident. I kept reading through the New Jedi Order series with the Yuuzhan Vong. Even accepted the torture of Jacen in New Jedi Order: *Traitor*. I finally stopped

# Reading Star Wars (cont)

reading in the following series when Jacen fell to the darkside. I suppose it was too difficult to accept the changes that were wrought in a favored character when I was younger.

I guess just knowing that Mara Jade dies was more than I could take. I read for the fun, the action, the love, the politics, and of course the sad moments of deaths and failure.  And not just the books. I read the comic of Luke and Mara Jade's wedding called *Union*. It branched me out into following art to tell the stories, something I hadn't tried before. Yet how could I miss out on that love story? And perhaps the tragic separation of Luke and Mara Jade in the later books were too much to continue reading.

Still with every book I did read I would finish it with three feelings: contentment, wanting to throw it in the trash (a rare event), or a feeling as I sit on my bed wanting more, unable or unwilling to wait for the next one. So I would spend an hour or so imagining what came next. Whether I ever read more, these books will always be a part of my young adult life.

# Friends from Fandoms

Custom crocheted dolls, forged from the fires of geekiness.

# Bella Dolce Couture Presents:

# STAR WARS DOLLS

Visit www.facebook.com/belladolcecouture for ordering information and new products

# i never wanted to be leia

## What Han Solo Taught Two Women About Gender and Sexuality

## A.J. O'Connell and Tamela Ritter

## Part One:

You know that old chestnut about James Bond: "Women want him and men want to be him?" I think that was also supposed to apply to Han Solo. He's got so many Bond characteristics: he works his way through the Galaxy, having adventures, slinging a blaster, wearing tight pants and a sexy sneer, putting his feet up on cantina tables, shooting first.

Women were supposed to want him. Men were supposed to want to be him. And because of this, I was deeply confused by him for years. I never wanted Han to save me, or kiss me, or say "I know" to me. Yet I was drawn to him, far more than I was drawn to any of the other characters. I paid more attention to his scenes. I knew his lines. I just wasn't attracted to him, and I could not understand that. It wasn't that I didn't find Harrison Ford attractive—I had a raging crush on Indiana Jones, after all—I just felt differently about Han. As late as college, when other women tried to bond with me over Han Solo, I would reluctantly admit to a crush I didn't really have on the character. Sometimes, I would convince myself I had one, because I must, right? Why else would I be obsessed by him?

As a kid, when I played Star Wars with my brother or friends, there weren't a lot of characters open to me, or at least I didn't think there were, because this was the '80s: girls were supposed to play girl characters; boys were supposed to play boy characters. When it came time to choose characters,

I never had a burning desire to yell, "I'm Princess Leia." It wasn't that I didn't like Leia. I did, and I still do. It was just that being her didn't appeal to me.

I let other girls play Leia. Instead, I made up my own character. She had a ship (my bed) and a comm (my Care Bears tape recorder) which played "transmissions" from the Death Star, and although she made a lot of brave pew-pew noises, the Death Star always ended up hauling her in with a tractor beam (because it's no fun if you get away without having to hide in the hold first). Even then—after many imaginary missions to the Death Star, and after creating a character in a high school drama class who was a sexy lady who piloted a plane, and had adventures ("On her own?" asked one girl in my class, "but who is her boyfriend?")—I didn't get it.

I credit gender-swapped cosplay for finally making my own feelings clear to me. One day I was browsing Facebook when I saw a photo of a female friend, dressed as Han Solo for a convention. I felt this little tendril of jealousy curl up within me, in exactly the way it never did when I saw Han and Leia kissing in the movies. But seeing my friend rocking her blaster at a con made me finally understand: *That's what I want*, I thought. That is what I've always wanted. I want to fly a broken-down ship with my best friend. I want to laugh at danger. I want an enemy as cool as Boba Fett.

But then, I thought back on my life, and saw that I've kind of had that, without all the blasters and spaceships. I've had a career where I didn't really have to follow many rules. I drive a car that's pretty Falcon-like in its breakdowns. I've got so many friends to have adventures with. Hell, my name is even Ann.

I never wanted Han Solo. I wanted to *be* him.

It's a little embarrassing that I didn't figure it out sooner, because it seems so simple: you should be able to be whoever you want, no matter your gender, race, or your sexuality. You can be drawn to a character without being limited by a crush on him or her.

Yes, Han Solo is a sexy beast. But that doesn't mean we all have to lust after him. We can be sexy beasts too, if we want.

# Part Two:

I have a distinct memory of walking out of the theater with stars in my eyes and only one thought in my mind. Han Solo. I also remember vividly looking at my younger sister who had the same expression and being horrified when she whispered in awe, "Luke Skywalker." My mind could not comprehend how we could see the same movie and she not see how superior Han was to Luke. It still baffles me.

I used to think I could tell a lot about a person by who they preferred, Luke or Han. But the world doesn't work like that and my sister soon got over her first crush. I never did.

I've put a lot of thought into Han Solo over the years. A lot. In fact, I've just recently come to terms with the fact that I'm not so much a Star Wars fan as I am a Han Solo fan. The movies without him mean very little to me. This occurred to me when I realized my problems with the prequel movies are far different than everyone else's.

And since I've had him in my life for as long as I've had memory, he's been my prototype for the characters I am drawn to in fiction and the characteristics I find myself most attracted to in real life.

They must be funny, that's a MUST, sarcasm is my go to, but just plain witty is a close second. They have to, at the very least, allude to a life lived beyond the story we're in, a shady past, a driving force all their own. They tend not to be the "hero" of the story; instead they are the hero's best friend, or even better, the anti-hero. They need to be the person who has their own agenda, who despite their better judgment, will eventually do the right thing, but maybe not for the "right" reasons. Of course having a roguish, wicked Harrison Ford grin doesn't hurt, but we can't have everything.

Still though, even with all the thought and devotion I've put into Han Solo, I never wanted to be Princess Leia. I never wanted to have that relationship.

My life would have made so much more sense so much earlier if I would have realized way back then that who I really wanted to be in the Star Wars universe was Chewbacca; the sexless side-kick. I just wanted to travel with Han, have shenanigans and some glorious banter that only we truly understand. And never, ever have sex.

Though, I might not have realized my true sexual identity—or lack of sexual desire—for longer than I'd like, I realize now that I've always subconsciously looked for the Hans that didn't want me to be their Leia, that would let me be their Chewie.

In my 20s I found a Han to have epic shenanigans with and I introduced him to my sister—his Princess Leia. Twenty-five years later, and we're still riding around in the Millennium Falcon having adventures, kicking ass. About a dozen years ago, I moved 3,000 miles away from them and found another Han—her name, Ann, was even close—and I've been her Chewie every since.

What Han taught me is that you can be attracted to people and characters in many different ways. There will always be characters you can relate to and they can always tell you things about yourself to help you on your journey. You just have to listen.

If you enjoyed this article, check out *Beware the Hawk*, found on Amazon and Goodreads.

Also, you can find the other half at www.tamelajritter.com where she blogs mostly about her day job, and being a reluctant Whovian.

# Brian Lacy

Graphic Artist

instagram: b.lacy0069

facebook: brianlacyart

http://Brian_lacy_art.com

# My Love For Star Wars

## Melissa Crawford-O'Brien

I was born the year *Star Wars*: Episode IV, *A New Hope* came out. I was three, when *The Empire Strikes Back* was released and when *Return of the Jedi* came out, I was six. I never saw the original movies in the theaters, but when they were re-released years later, I lined up with my friends to see it on the big screen. Even remastered, I was mesmerized from start to finish, even having watched the films hundreds of times!

I can remember from an early age being enthralled with Star Wars. In first grade, we had puppets of Princess Leia, Luke Skywalker and Darth Vader. At free time, my best friend Amanda, and I used to fight over who would be Princess Leia and who would be Darth Vader. She usually won! But our shared love of the movie and of the characters was one of things that bonded me to her. The other thing was that my mother loved the movies as much as we did.

She loved all of the movies, even episodes I, II, and III. I remember going with her to the video store and renting the movies, over and over, and over again. I was wondrous at the fact that this entire universe—the characters, the story lines, the Millennium Falcon, etc. were from the mind of the creative genius, George Lucas.

I heard a story once where, when *Star Wars: Episode IV, A New Hope* premiered, Mr. Lucas was sure it would be a flop. He left his hotel and just drove around. He happened to come across a midnight showing of the movie and was stunned when he saw people who were lined up around the block, waiting to get into see his movie! That was enough to spur him to continue telling the story. And I am so glad he did.

One of my very favorite scenes in the entire collection, all six, was in *A New Hope*, when Han Solo, and Luke Skywalker were dressed up as storm troopers to rescue Princess Leia. When they end up getting into a shootout with the actual Imperial guards, the officer hits the alarm, before falling, so Han rushes to the com-link system to re-assure them that everything is fine. The line he delivers:

"Uh… had a slight weapons malfunction. But, uh, everything's perfectly all right now. We're fine. We're all fine here, now, thank you. How are you?" is pure gold! I found out years later that Harrison Ford purposely didn't read his lines for that scene and ad libbed it, so it would appear real. That fact endeared the scene even more to me because it showed the level of commitment the actors had to the characters they were playing, making it real for the audience.

But my main reason for loving *Star Wars* is that George Lucas had a dream and regardless of what anyone else thought or said, he worked to achieve the vision he had in his head. That's one of the reasons why I persevere as a writer, because Mr. Lucas inspired me to never give up on my dreams.

As we approach December of 2015, my level of excitement to see *Star Wars:* Episode VII, *The Force Awakens* grows. This time though, it's bittersweet for me. My mother passed away two years ago, so we won't be able to physically share watching this movie together and talking about our favorite parts after.

I won't be at the midnight premiere for the movie. I will probably even wait for a couple of weeks after it opens before I go to see it. But I know that the night I do see it, on the big screen, I won't be alone. On one side of me will be my best friend, and on the other will be my husband and, in a locket that is always around my neck, and in my heart, will be my mother. She will be there with me, watching the characters we love, and the magic, unfold yet again!

**Mazikeen Studios**
Handmade Fandom-Centric Jewelry

Custom orders welcome!
Multi-fandom jewelry is a specialty.
Contact me for a charm list for you fandom.

Follow me on Facebook: MazikeenStudios
See new designs here: www.mazikeenstudios.com
Shop online at my etsy store: Mazikeenstudios

# Star Wars Memories
## I. Anne Wooley

The year 1977, May; I remember standing in the long line around the back of the University City Movie Theater with my best friend Christina Westervelt. We had been wanting to see this film since we first heard about it. Star Wars was different conceptually to most movies than had been out previously. I was kind of sheltered as a child as well, so I had not seen many films that weren't Disney related.

Back then, the movie theater would have a line out the door and around the building. They only showed maybe two movies at a time, this was long before the multiplex was born. So we had to wait to get in. But it was so worth it. I loved every bit of it. It captured our twelve year old imaginations and we were mesmerized by it. The special effects were awesome—though compared to now, are somewhat amateurish—but the technology was barely in its infancy.

When we got out, it was like we had never seen a movie before. We promised each other, we would see it again...as many times as our parents would let us. And we did see it more than a couple. It invaded our imaginations, waking and sleeping. We started telling each other of our "dreams," and wound stories around the characters and ourselves. Funny how I was "writing" even then! I know for my part, I was making them up...not sure about my friend. We also put other shows we liked in with *Star Wars*...like *Emergency*. The dreams/stories evolved until she and I were Darth Vader's daughters, and girlfriends to Johnny (though I'm pretty sure she was the one who put herself with him mostly).

We even put together a dance routine with some light sabers and costumes for our 8th grade talent show. I remember how we practiced down in my family's basement, and she was better at gymnastics than I, so she did all of the fancier moves that I couldn't.

# Memories (cont)

We had the soundtrack on 33 rpm, vinyl...yes, I am that old! We would practice for hours, and she was a harsh taskmistress, but I persevered. We didn't win....but we had a lot of fun doing it.

The following year, we added Margaret Sheppard to the mix. She was a fan like we were, so we decided on nicknames. Chris was the irascible, bitchy one, so she was Chewbacca, Margaret loved to whistle, and as she was kinda shaped like him at the time (though not now), became R2D2, and I, being the long winded, talker extraordinaire, became C-3PO. These have stuck to present day, by the way.

One of the things I liked about *Star Wars*, it showed that girls could be heroes too. That they could hold their own, and even save the day. Leia Organa was the woman who every little girl looked up to. Even I, who was a tomboy and eschewed all things girlish, looked up to her.

Why I think it grabbed hold of the public the way it did, was not just because of the strong characters, it was the story. The story of a young boy yearning for adventure, torn between staying with his aunt and uncle, and going off to the academy to learn how to fight in the rebellion against the Empire. His friends are already there, and he is resentful of having to stay behind. Then he meets Obi Wan Kenobi, someone who is mentioned in a video message that is in R2D2.

He goes back to his uncle's farms and finds them dead. He has nothing to keep him there, and takes off with Ben.

It's the story of Luke becoming part of a major life changing event. A huge fight for the freedom of the galaxy, something that is so much bigger than himself, so overwhelming for a farm boy, that we feel for him, and even more importantly root for him. The characters he meets along the way, Han and Chewie, and Princess Leia. You have a growing camaraderie between Luke and Han, who become like brothers. The transformation of the characters as they struggle to survive and defeat the Empire. Basically the fight between good and evil. Little by little, Luke figures out that he is not just a normal human with no special abilities. On the contrary, he really does have powers, that he is part of the Force.

The story actually starts with Episodes IV, V, and VI. I look upon this trilogy like a hamburger. *A New Hope*, is the top of the bun, that it holds the meat in, that it is where you hold the sandwich. It's the biggest part and it introduces the basic structure of the story, and introduces us to all the main characters. In Empire, we delve more deeply into the story, the stakes are upped, they are brought to the attention of the Emperor, and Darth Vader. It's the hamburger. They begin to make a difference and rally the support of the Rebel Alliance. Secrets are revealed, and the bad things happen to the main characters. In *Return of the Jedi*, the ending of the story, we see a wrap up of pretty much everything, and we do see the redemption of Darth Vader. It's the bottom thinner slice of the bun, the climax of the story.

Over the years, I've seen all the movies in the series, the technology got better, and then Lucas put out the remade versions, with updated technology. I did enjoy them, and some of the new stuff looked amazing. However, It kind of did lose the feeling that I originally enjoyed, but that might have been my perceptions changing as I got older. Though the best part was the trailer for the new revamped movies.

The familiar logo of Lucasfilms turning color, the sure sign it is a *Star Wars* Film Trailer...and the voice over, "If you have only seen *Star Wars* on a screen like this...." and a small TV appears, the size of the tv gets a bit larger, and you see a star destroyer on its tiny screen. Then the voiceover continues..."...just wait until you see it like this!" And then the tv disappears and the screen explodes with the size of the destroyer, majestic and scary as it flies through space. The the music comes in. I really broke down and cried with the immensity of the movie trailer. I really never had been moved by a trailer. Seeing it on the big screen though, was so much more impressive. I quite literally about peed my pants when I saw it.

I hope the new *Star Wars* movie, coming out December 2015, isn't going to be a bust, but seeing the old cast in it makes me feel better about it. Looking at the trailers, and the online stuff, I'm really getting excited. Why isn't it December yet?

# C.C. Lynch

www.cclynchbooks.com

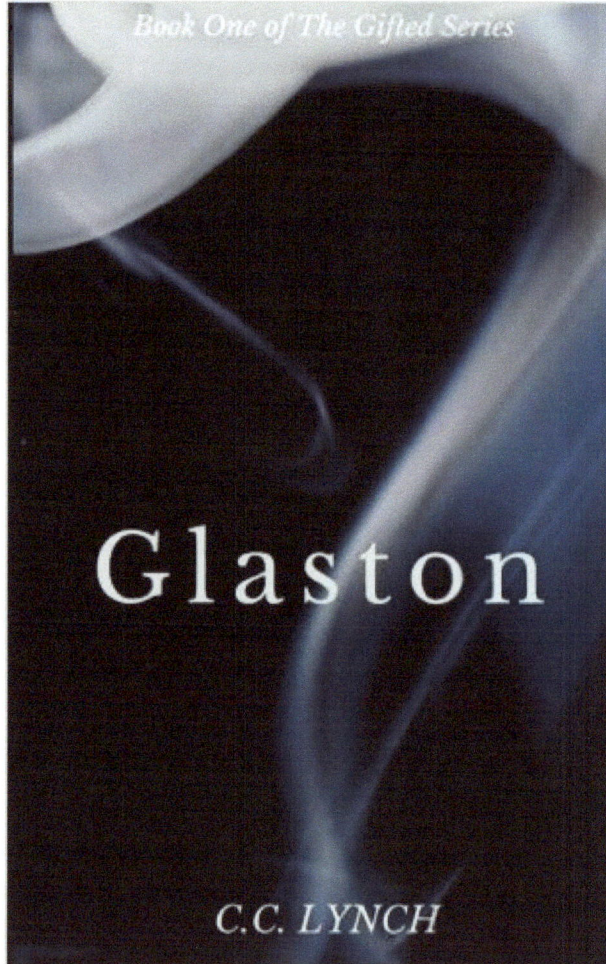

Book One of The Gifted Series

# Glaston

C.C. LYNCH

*I saw you die.*

Four words scribbled onto a piece of paper from a fellow telepath are only the beginning of a chain of events no one saw coming. Abrielle soon finds herself at Glaston Academy, a school filled with gifted minds where she must learn to fine tune her innate abilities. When she discovers that telepathy is not her only skill she becomes the target of a malicious organization looking to exploit her rare gift by any means necessary. With only a reticent roommate, brooding mentor, and the handsome man of her visions to turn to, can she survive her first year at Glaston?

# Rebel Scum

## Brian Voris

As my wife will attest, I am a huge gamer. It's my hobby and I spend a great deal of time playing games of all kinds. As a kid, however, there was only one thing that really drew my interest – Star Wars. I really started to get into video games in the late 80's and early 90's, when the NES, SNES, and Sega Genesis were all the rage. I had seen the movie trilogy, of course, and was really excited when *Super Star Wars* was released in 1992. That's right, *Super Star Wars*—since it was the Super NES, every video game that came out for it had to be Super. Unfortunately for me, my parents wouldn't even let me have a console. But we did have a computer; Dad needed one for his work.

We did have a few games for the computer, but not many. There was a *Jeopardy!* game, and *Wheel of Fortune* because my parents liked game-shows, but nothing that really held my interest. But then *TIE Fighter* came out for PC. My favorite part of *Star Wars* had always been the space battles, and while I would later learn that an X-Wing video game had come out previously (these were the days before the Internet, so information on video games was relegated to magazines), the first one I saw on the store shelf was *TIE Fighter*. I immediately started saving my allowance to purchase the game.

The game came on like a billion floppy disks, as these were the days before the CD-ROM became the preferred media. These were also the days before Windows 95, so we ran DOS as the main operating system. Windows 3.1 was on the computer, but it wasn't used for games, mostly. You'd boot into DOS, insert the first floppy disk for the game, and follow the instruction manual to load the game up on the computer. With this game, I had to swap floppy disks out numerous times before it even loaded to the title screen.

When the title did finally load, I was ecstatic. This was Star Wars, and I was about to have some epic space battles! The game loads into a "concourse"

# Rebel Scum (cont)

view of the inside of an Imperial ship as the main menu, where different doors lead to different game options. There were even little animations that would run if you left the screen idle for a little bit. This was exactly what I imagined the interior of a Star Destroyer must have looked like for a pilot about to go out on a mission. I immediately started up the first mission.

I immediately crashed and burned. I hadn't read the manual or done any of the training, and the distinct lack of a joystick caused me innumerable problems when trying to maneuver the fighter. Plus, the lack of shields on a standard TIE fighter meant that I was a sitting duck when I encountered my first group of Rebel Scum. So I went back to the manual, read about the speed, attitude, and fire controls, and went through the built-in training slalom until I got it right. Then I tried the mission again.

The first mission in *TIE Fighter* is a trade inspection mission. Honestly, before *TIE Fighter* I never even thought of the Empire doing this kind of stuff. See, the Empire wasn't just some evil force to be reckoned with, it was actually a functioning government. And functioning governments do things like trade inspection to catch smugglers, illegal goods, and of course Rebel Scum. The mistake I had made the first time around was that I set a course and flew right at the different groups of ships in order to scan them. That put me right in the firing-line of the rebel lasers when I approached their ships, and being in a measly TIE fighter, I was toast. This time, having mastered the attitude controls, I carefully maneuvered around the side of each group, and scanned them from behind, and slightly above. That way, I was able to avoid enemy fire, and quickly destroy or disable any smuggler or rebel ships I came across before they had the chance to turn around and destroy me.

My first success! Elated, I continued to progress through the single-player campaign. There were escort missions, attack missions, any mission a TIE fighter might've flown. I was hooked. Then came x-wing versus TIE fighter, which introduced online multi-player.

How would my skills stack up against other players?

Quite well, as it turned out. I was pretty evenly skilled with everyone I played against, and it was great fun. Real people did things a lot differently from

AI opponents, and it took a little getting used to. No longer could I get behind an opponent and blast away, other players were much more skilled at evasive manoeuvres.

I had to learn to work with my wingmen to bring down more skilled enemies. Since these were the days of dial-up still, this meant communication was kept at a minimum—no voice chat. Since you were busy piloting a fighter, there was also no typing. What we had to work with was a set of pre defined messages that could be sent with the press of a particular key on the keyboard. There was a button to call for help, one for "follow me" and one for "attack my target."

All this meant that everybody had to be on the same page. Prior to a match, my friends and I work out whose commands we would follow, what formations we'd attempt to fly in, and what strategy we'd try to use. We won more often than we lost.

I played each successive iteration of the X-wing and TIE fighter games, and was sad when there was no sequel after *X-wing Alliance*, but of course those weren't the only *Star Wars* games. They were just the most memorable for me, and they played an important role in my development as a gamer and as a person.

Star Wars games kick-started my love of losing myself in a different world, in the kind of immersive world that video games can offer. Whatever the rest of the world thought of video games, they helped me learn to think of different scenarios and possibilities, to put myself in someone else's shoes. They helped me develop teamwork and communication skills.

But mostly they helped me learn how to defeat Rebel Scum.

# Kinda Sorta in the Fandom

## Nicole Slazinski

My introduction to *Star Wars* was seeing the remastered version of Episode IV at the Regal Cinema movie theater. I remember liking it, along with Episodes V and VI, but I was never a huge "Omg, this is the best thing ever!" type of fan. (Though I do confess, I always enjoyed the awkward relationship between Luke and Vader.) Episodes I, II, and III were certainly… interesting. Though I was indifferent to them, I could see why the die-hard fans were so disappointed.

It has only been recently where I've been sucked into the Star Wars fandom. Though I've never read any of the books, and I still don't understand the huge appeal of Boba Fett, I consider myself a fan. Lately, I've been finding myself excited when walking into a department store to be greeted by Star Wars merchandise. So what's changed?

Being married to a Star Wars fan has certainly helped. My husband was very patient with me, answering all of my annoying questions as I re-watched episodes IV, V, and VI. As I was viewing the original movies, I tried paying attention to the little details, taking in all of the characters and their background stories, and just like that, I became hooked.

Then came *Star Wars: The Old Republic* (SWTOR). My husband needed a break from his current game, so he purchased a subscription for SWTOR. I had always wanted to try a multi-player online (MMO); the only one I had tried previously was *Lord of the Rings*, and I quickly lost interest. He was really enjoying the game and suggested that I try it out. It was only fifteen dollars a month, so if the game wasn't for me, I could just unsubscribe.

As this game was my first MMO, I was utterly confused at first. Like with the movies, my husband was super patient with me, and eventually I got the feel for the game. The game takes place 3,500 years before the movies, giving the developers a lot of room for creativity.

You explore a variety of planets, such as familiar ones like Tatooine, Alderaan, and Hoth, as well as some new planets. There is a huge variety of characters to choose from, some species from the movies, some completely new. The game has the familiarity of the Star Wars universe, with the classic Republic vs. The Empire rivalry, but it also has its own unique touch.

At this time, I've created three characters. A Smuggler (my first character), a Bounty Hunter, and a Sith. I also created a Jedi, being enthralled with the thought of being able to slash my villains with my own lightsaber. However, the Sith character has a lightsaber as well, and I've been enjoying that storyline so much that my Jedi character continues to sit at Level 1. Plus, playing a Sith gives me the perspective from the Empire where the Republics are considered the villains, a unique twist I quite enjoy. There are very few games where you actually get to play the villain. Being someone who is typically viewed as sweet and innocently minded, I love playing a villain because it's totally different from me. Though I must admit, I did have trouble killing innocent people at first, which of course humored my husband. Actually, I still have trouble making my character do cruel things. I have to keep reminding myself that I actually do want the Empire to win victoriously, and the Republic to suffer in miserable defeat.

In conclusion, that is how I became a fan of the Star Wars universe. I wouldn't say I'm a die-hard fan by any means, because there is still so much to learn and the fandom is overwhelmingly large. However, I at least get the basic gist, and SWOTR has made me feel like a part of the Star Wars universe.

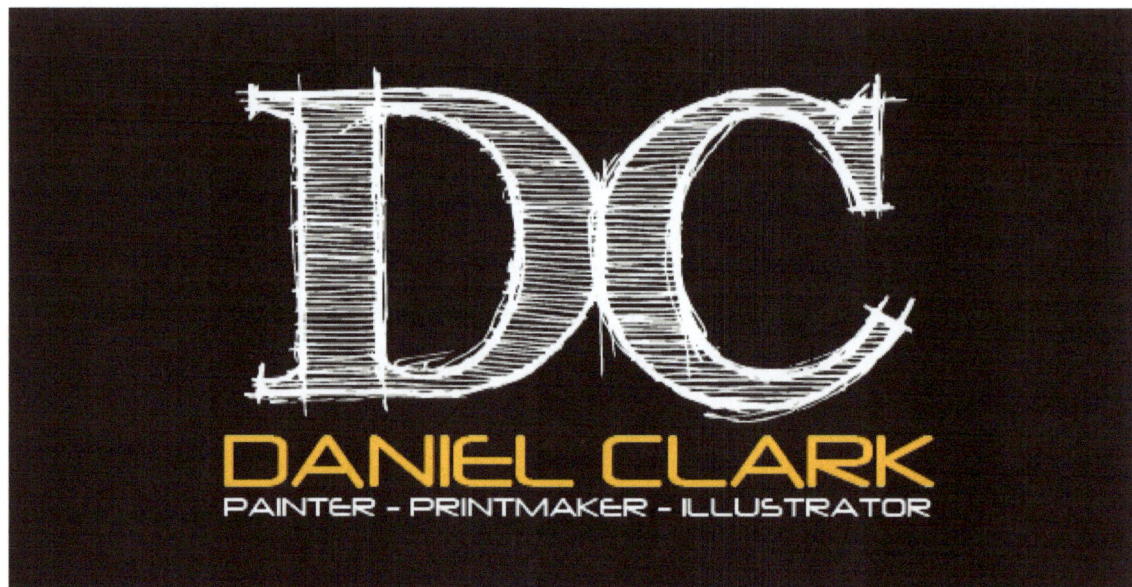

# Kate and Star Wars

## Tom Boone

As a young boy of five when *Star Wars* was originally released, I grew up at the perfect time to enjoy the films and the toys. I collected every figure including the final Power of the Force line, bought comics from spinner racks at the local pharmacy, got the glasses at Burger King and occasionally my father would bring home a pack of cards or stickers from High's. I recall my early days as an "original" *Star Wars* fan with great fondness. But unquestionably the happiest period of my life as a Star Wars fan and collector was the period between 2008 and 2012, when my daughter Kate, thanks to *Star Wars: The Clone Wars*, joined in the fun.

Having collected for thirty years, and having a nice—though limited—space to display my collection, I wanted to sit out on *The Clone Wars* when the merchandising wave began in 2008. I felt the six movies was a good stopping point and with the cartoon likenesses of *The Clone Wars* action figures, it seemed easy enough to draw the line. Still, I enjoyed the series immensely. The movie, *Star Wars: The Clone Wars* would be the first *Star Wars* film that my wife and daughter and I would see in the theater together. Kate was five years old at the time, about the same age as I when I first saw Star Wars.

As it turned out, the new figures were too cool to ignore entirely. I bought the hero figures, Anakin, Obi-Wan, R2-D2, etc., but called it quits at that. I also bought the trading cards from Topps, including the sticker set and tins. I wound up with hundreds of extra stickers so I gave them to Kate to give to her friends at kindergarten. Kate enjoyed being generous with the stickers. Soon the entire class was inundated with images of Captain Rex and Anakin and General Grievous and I was politely asked by the teacher to stop sending Star Wars stickers to school with Kate!

The following Christmas, despite my pleas for no *The Clone Wars* toys, Kate bought an Asaaj Ventress figure for me, which, again, was too cool to ignore. I quickly justified buying the main villains, which led to all the characters

# Kate (cont)

that were never before made, like Whorm Loathesome, and suddenly nearly everything in the Clone Wars line. Father's Day and Valentine's Day and my birthday were filled with Clone Wars gifts from Kate like the blue ATT, Goji, Quinlan Vos (her favorite,) and a Yoda finger puppet she found at a craft show. My excitement was apparently contagious to Kate as she pined for an Ahsoka Tano figure, which even a year or so on, was still tough to find.

Soon Kate did get her own Ahsoka and she began her own infatuation with *Star Wars*. We watched *The Clone Wars* together every week. When I couldn't be there because of work, we'd DVR the show to watch it together the next day. We fought with lightsabers and clone trooper foam dart guns in the basement surrounded by my Star Wars collection, occasionally knocking over an action figure or two or a phalanx of stormtroopers in the process! She attended DC Star Wars Collector Club meetings with me and even joined me on a road trip to the JediCon in Wheeling, West Virginia. We also decided that we could run our own convention and make it a benefit for her school. We drove home from West Virginia dreaming up ideas about how to make our convention the best we could. For the next three years, with her inspiration, I organized the ANS Sci-Fi & Comic Con, raising several thousand dollars for her school.

Kate's enthusiasm began to rub off on me too, as I found myself collecting the Star Wars equivalent of Squinkies, Star Wars Fighter Pods. Kate and my wife went to the store one day retuning with a couple of these deformed, rubbery little figurines. Once again, I thought I'd try to get only the main characters. But once you get Bossk you realize everyone is a main character in *Star Wars*! I bought the entire series, and nearly every one for Kate, too. My collection wouldn't be nearly as fun without Kate. Her *Star Wars* collection grew as well, as she enjoyed the Hasbro dolls as well as the action figures. She would swap out heads and hands, change capes and clothes and helmets and add weird accessories to the figures. In short, she did what a kid is actually supposed to do with her toys—she PLAYED with them!

One of the biggest highlights of this period was getting the opportunity to see the first Savage Opress arc on a big movie screen. I don't remember how

I learned about the screening, but I scored two tickets. Kate was almost eight at that time. The theater wasn't in the best part of town by any stretch, but I took a shot. The theater was on the top floor of a huge shopping mall with an enormous escalator held up only on faith, I'm sure. It seriously looked to be an engineering impossibility to me, certainly not for the squeamish. But we made it up and got in line.

Stormtroopers were around, of course, an R2-D2 from the local DC R2 Builders Club and a few guys from the DC Star Wars Collectors Club, too. Kate and I waited patiently for about an hour. I should note that the hour of waiting in line is why my wife demurred and chose not to accompany me to the screening. But it turned out to be worth the wait. We were each given a souvenir ticket and a few other bits of swag and soon we were in the theater watching the most unlikely *Star Wars* story I'd seen at that point. Ventress rejected, Night Sister witches, weird magicks, a new monstrous Darth Maul-type character, awesome lightsaber battles. I leaned over to Kate and said, "I can't believe this! Isn't this great?"

Like me, Kate was transfixed. "Yes," she smiled.

The only disappointment was that it did have to end. But when we left the theater, more gifts awaited us in the form of Savage t-shirts and incredible posters. I was amazed at the generosity of Lucasfilm for presenting such an event. Kate and I had so much fun together that night. It was the most memorable night I had as a Star Wars fan, watching *The Clone Wars* Monster arc in a theater with my little girl. I got the poster framed. It's an homage to monster movie posters of the thirties. A beautiful piece (if something with Savage Opress' demonic, horned head on it could be called beautiful!) with great, unexpected little details like Savage's village and Mother Talzin working her 'magicks.' Every time I look at that creepy poster, which hangs on the stairway leading to my collection, I think about that impossibly happy night.

Everything culminated in the whirlwind crescendo of Star Wars Celebration 6 in Orlando Florida in the summer of 2012. Kate and my wife and I took the train to the Sunshine State for one of the best vacations ever. We stayed in a fabulous hotel near the Orlando Convention Center and only a short

# Kate (cont)

cab ride to Disney World. None of us are fans of the Diz, in particular, though we appreciate the artistry of many of the classic movies like Bambi and Snow White. But it must be said that Disney World is just about the nicest theme park we've ever been too. All the food was good, everything was clean and neat and there was plenty of Star Wars and Star Tours stuff for me to buy!

Kate and I waited patiently in line for our Build-A-Droids. My wife, always averse to all lines, patiently waited outside on a bench. While I carefully selected each droid part to ensure they matched and had the best possible paint apps, Kate built crazy, multi-colored, mixed up droids. I went to Celebration alone on the first day, while the girls went off to Epcot. The next day, the three of us rolled into the Celebration together. Kate searched for a Darth Krayt figure and I an Ahsoka figure in her updated costume, among countless other items. We were both successful. Kate insisted we wear costumes. So for the first time and last time ever, I wore a costume, dressing as Han Solo. My beautiful wife dressed in THE gold bikini and Kate in customized blue-sashed Jedi robes. The costumes alone took up an entire bag of luggage!

But like the Monster arc in the theater or Kate's mom in the gold bikini, all good things must come to an end. Life must go on in a normal, non-gold bikini way, sometimes with a few disappointments along the way. Two months after the heady bliss of Celebration 6, George Lucas announced he was selling Star Wars to the Diz. And while many fanboys and Lucas-haters cheered saying, "Look what Disney did with the Avengers," Kate wisely lamented, "They'll probably put a dog in it." Sadly, she was right, from a certain point of view. The wretched dross from the Diz called Star Wars Rebels features a curmudgeonly belligerent and disobedient droid called Chopper that's as obnoxious as any scruffy family dog in any sickly sweet family adventure movie the Diz has ever made.

As their first official act as the new owners of the Star Wars franchise, the Diz cancelled *The Clone Wars*, cementing my disdain for the company.

As the final episodes led to the series' melancholy end, I could see Kate's interest in *Star Wars* was passing, too. She still enjoyed it, she still liked her toys and politely smiled when I enthused about new additions to my collection. But new things were coming into her life like manga and Minecraft and horses. As we watched the last episode and watched Ahsoka leave the temple, I couldn't help but feeling sad not just about the character, or the criminally unnecessary ending of the series, but for the end of a great era in the relationship between Kate and I. Of course we still have fun together and go places and look through comic and antique shops together and even play *The Clone Wars* Xbox game together. But for five years, we were co-conspirators, in the thick of a grand adventure in Star Wars fandom. Thank you for that wonderful, special time, Kate. I'll never forget it.

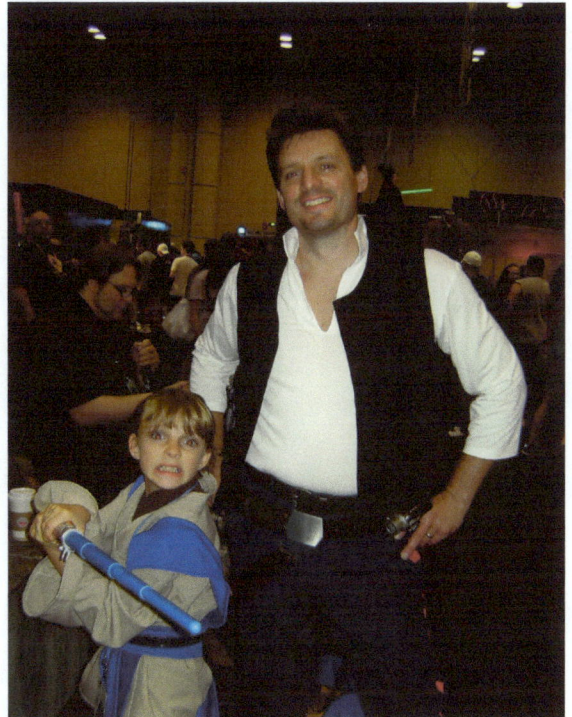

# Tom's Collection of Awesome

Editor's Note:

The next few pages will feature an awesome Star Wars collection by Tom Boone. I first met Tom at Awesome Con in Washington DC. He was manning the DC Star Wars Collector's Club booth at the con. I was passing fliers for this project and stopped to speak with him. He seemed excited about the project and promised to send us a contribution. He sent us a couple of pictures of him and his daughter in Star Wars costumes and a cute story about sharing his love of Star Wars with her. As I was putting this project together and sending out acceptance letters, I noticed in Tom's bio that he had been collecting Star Wars stuff since 1978. I thought that was pretty neat and asked if he would submit pictures of his collection. He was more than thrilled to share his collection. He sent me a link to his blog that featured his entire collection. I wasn't prepared for the enormity of the collection. I was, and still am, in awe. He gave me permission to pull photos from his blog to use, but I had a difficult time picking and choosing the best ones. In fact, I didn't choose. It was impossible. I am including all of them so that everyone can see how amazing his collection actually is. Please note that the photos in the next section belong to Tom Boone and are used with permission. Enjoy!

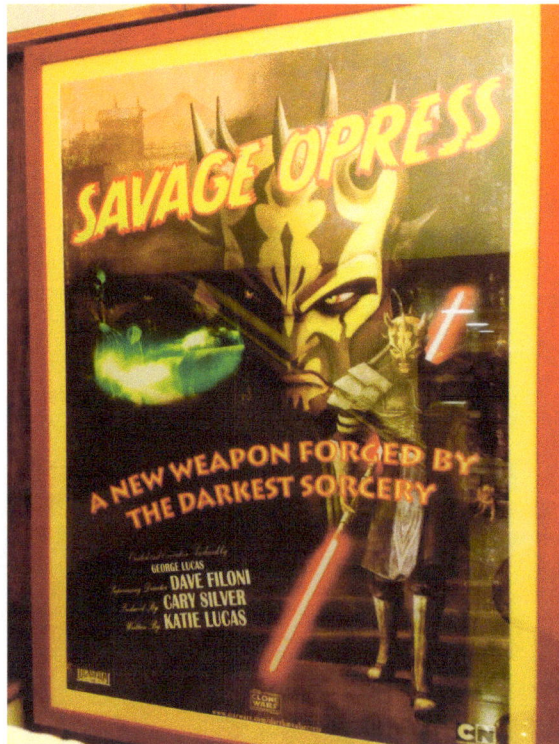

THE FIRST
STAR WARS
1977
1987
TEN YEARS
Brotherhood of Jedi Knights
RETURN OF THE JEDI
STAR WARS
STAR WARS 30
EMPIRE STRIKES BACK
STAR WARS LUCASFILM FAN CLUB
EMPIRE STRIKES BACK 30
BANTHA TRACKS
DARTH VADAR LIVES
REBELSCUM
MOS EISLEY SPACEPORT
STAR WARS
EMPIRE STRIKES BACK
LUCASFILM FAN CLUB

FOR TOM—
ALL MY BEST!
2-16-13

STAR WARS

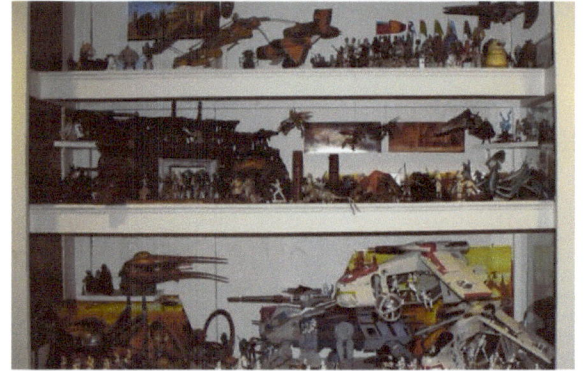

# Martin Wilsey

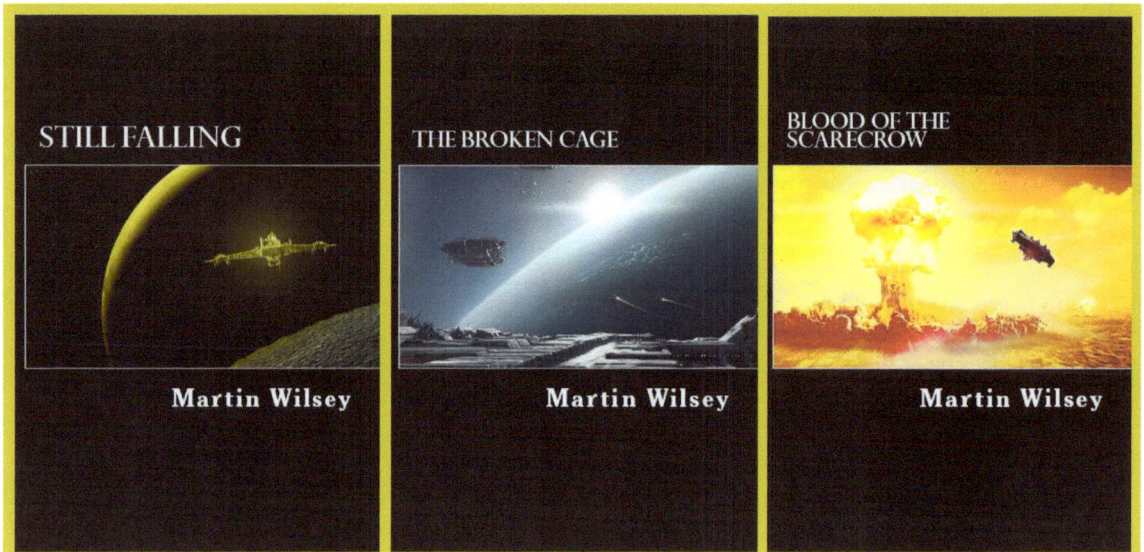

STILL FALLING
Martin Wilsey

THE BROKEN CAGE
Martin Wilsey

BLOOD OF THE SCARECROW
Martin Wilsey

Martin Wilsey is a writer, hunter, photographer, rabble rouser, father, friend, marksman, story teller, frightener of children, carnivore, engineer, fool, philosopher, cook and madman. He and his wife Brenda live in Virginia where, just to keep him off the streets, he works as a research scientist for a government funded think tank. For more information, check out his author page on Amazon.

# Star Wars Mom

## Amanda M. Greene

*Star Wars* played an important roll in my young life. I remember when I was a kid, playing with older brother's Star Wars toys. He had an X-Wing, the Millennium Falcon, and a TIE fighter. We were always chasing each other around the house with the ships. It was even more fun when my older sister came to visit. She lived with our grandmother and visited in the summer. With the three of us running around the house playing Star Wars, or trying to, we sounded like a herd of elephants—noisy elephants when we began bickering about who shot who, and who was supposed to be "dead." Our mother would reach the point where she would kick us outside. We all enjoyed *Star Wars*, even though my sister is more of a *Star Trek* nerd. We would gather all our blankets and pillows in the living room and pop the tape in the VCR and have a *Star Wars* night.

Fast forward a few years. I now have a five year old son. I wanted to introduce him to this series since I loved it so much, but I didn't know how he would take it. We had been seeing more and more Star Wars merchandise as well as television ads because of the new movie and he began to get curious, especially when it came to lighsabers. So I made the decision to have a movie night with him. We started with episode I. He was okay with it as well as episodes II and III. I was a little crestfallen since he didn't seem to be too interested. I thought maybe I should not finish and wait until he was a little older, but started the next movie in the series.

# star wars Mom (cont)

He was enthralled. He saw Luke Skywalker and Darth Vader and he was hooked. When he finished *Empire Strikes Back*, he looked at me and said, "Mom! That was amazing!" Since that moment, he has not talked about anything but Star Wars. Some days he puts on his Darth Vader mask and pretends to be fighting Jedi. Other days, he will put a blanket on his head, like a Jedi robe, and pretend to be fighting stormtroopers. There are Star Wars decals on my walls. Star Wars toys all over the house. He has asked for a Star Wars shirt for every day of the week. His lizards are even named Luke and Boba. I love to watch him play and to see his imagination run wild. It is never a dull moment with him. I'm so very glad to be able to share this with him. Being a Star Wars mom is hard work, but I wouldn't trade it for anything.

# Starla Huchton
## Author and Designer

A geek of all trades, Starla Huchton has been crafting stories in various genres since 2007. She is a three-time finalist for Parsec Awards for her podcast fiction work, and was the first place winner for Science Fiction & Fantasy in the Sandy competition in 2012. Her work spans science fiction, fantasy, New Adult Romance, Young Adult titles, Steampunk, Contemporary, and various other varieties of stories. She is greedy and likes all the genres!

When not writing, Starla trains three Minions, a black lab, and a military husband whilst designing book covers for independent authors and publishers at DesignedByStarla.com.

For more information about her books, check out her website at www.starlahuchton.com

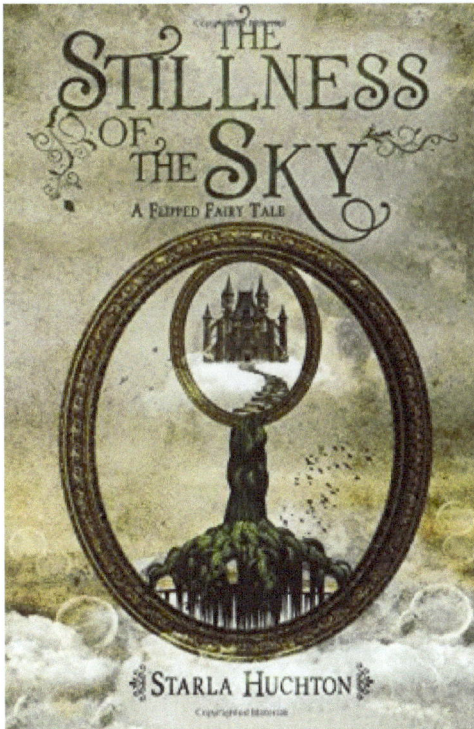

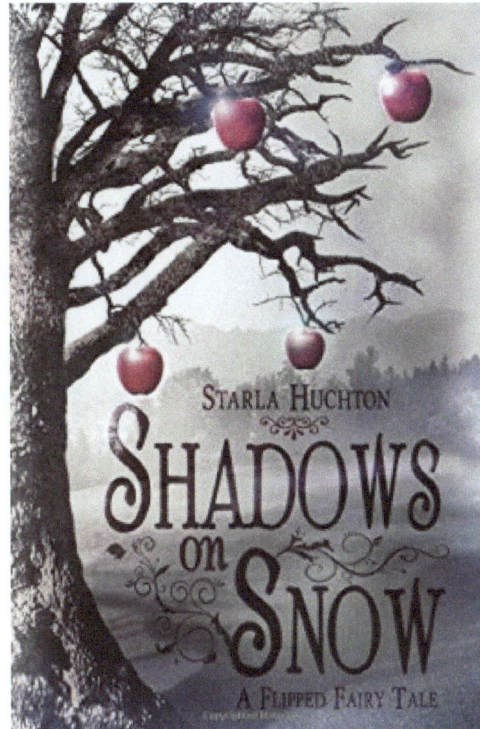

# a mind on the force

## chris saldana

What if I were to tell you, dear fellow fan, that one of the greatest Force Schools in all of the Star Wars universe has had naught but scant references in a single video game series and a handful of books? Welcome to the world of a Jal Shey fan, like myself. The Jal Shey are a Force tradition that exists within the Star Wars universe, and for what very little has been shown of them, they are quite possibly the most fascinating tradition.

Part of the reason they haven't been given a full showing is obvious, and totally understandable: the Jedi and their story are the heart and soul of the Star Wars universe. Their main opponents, the Sith, are born of an offshoot of the Jedi. Much of the major events that drive the action that we love so much within the Star Wars Universe is based, directly or indirectly, on the Jedi and their relationship with that great power within that universe known as The Force.

But for almost all of its existence, The Force is treated with this quasi-religious reverence. The Jedi seek to be one with it. The Sith wish to bend it to their will. And The Force, in some form or fashion, exists as a real thing within the universe. You see it in the intuition of the Force users, the indirect touch of The Force being used to throw large objects, to guide lightsabers to defend against plasma bolts, to the now legendary "proton torpedo in the Death Star thermal exhaust port" shot that made *A New Hope* so memorable. It exists within the universe. So who would be curious about this power, one who would want to study the Force not as a priest examines his faith but as a scientist studies the fundamental forces of the universe.

Those scientists are the Jal Shey. Described within the *Knights of the Old Republic* game series as a collection of Force users who study the Force academically. The Jal Shey have the same gifts as the Jedi and Sith and apply a lens not often seen within the Star Wars universe: that of critical thought. There is very little of science within the Star Wars universe, as this is effectively a universe built from pulp action origins. Science fact often took a backseat to the story of amazing action and pulse-pounding thrills. Amazing dogfights between TIE fighters and X-wings take a front seat before things like physics and esoteric questions, but there have been rather interesting points made within the Star Wars universe. The whole galaxy is riddled with lost ships, colonies, and even whole civilizations that have had a massive influence upon the galaxy. From the myriad failed Sith Empires to the Taung, there are dozens if not hundreds of civilizations that existed within the universe with a massive amount of relics and places of power within The Force left behind after their fall. One of the few confirmed things about the Jal Shey, from the *Knights of the Old Republic Campaign Guide*, is that they would not only travel to these places but were also militant in their stances.

What this brings to mind is a concept that works in as expansive a universe as the Star Wars one: the Jal Shey are aggressive defenders of lost lore and recovering lost lore from before that point. Militant academics don't look like Jedi, or even Sith, but more like a character from another Lucasfilm franchise: it is a Force school with the soul of Indiana Jones. And the idea of a whole Force School that exists to recover old artifacts and lore with similar pulp origins as *Star Wars* is based off of works amazingly well in a shared universe. Where it works best is as a counterpoint to the Jedi and their reverence to the Force, one where the pragmatism of the Jal Shey works as a mirror the Jedi aesthetics as well as being a bridging point between the grimy underbelly of Star Wars and the nobility that births the Jedi.

In mentioning counterpoints, there is another one that is shown in just how the Jal Shey have a reputation. Within the same book as the point above, it's revealed that the Jal Shey have existed as counterparts to the Jedi for over 4000 years, with a similar (albeit as mentioned more academic) preference for the light side of The Force. They were contemporaries of the Jedi during the time of Revan, and within the *Imperial Commandos: 501st* novel it was revealed that they were still in existence during The Dark Times which take place between the third and fourth movies.

So what does it mean for the Star Wars Galaxy as a whole? It means that not only are the Jal Shey around, but they have been a constant within the Galaxy. They are a Force School that is not only contemporary to the Jedi, but not an offshoot of it. Most of the Force Schools shown within the Star Wars universe besides the Jedi, such as the Sith or the Zeison Sha, are offshoots of the Jedi in some form or another. There are some obvious examples of independent Force schools, like the Voss Mystics or the Aing-Tii monks, but often those are tied with a distinctly alien culture.

The Jal Shey, however, have shown to be active within the Galaxy. Again, the *Knights of the Old Republic Campaign Guide* talks of the Jal Shey acting as diplomats that rival the Jedi in terms of skill, combined with a mastery of the art of debate that even exceeded the Jedi themselves. They should have a very obvious presence within the galaxy, even if they don't have the numbers of the Jedi. They even have ranks amongst themselves, in much the same way the Jedi do. They have neophytes instead of padawans, advisers instead of knights, and mentors instead of masters, but they clearly have a large enough structure that it requires differentiation. This means that they should have numbers enough to be noticeable within galactic society as a whole. Couple that with them being on par with the Jedi themselves as diplomats? Impressive. Most impressive.

And speaking of being on par to the Jedi, there is one more thing about the Jal Shey again revealed in the *Knights of the Old Republic Campaign Guide*: they heavily favor the light side of the Force. This provides a rather interesting point within the Star Wars Universe: The Jedi are often treated as moral and beyond reproach, and any sort of criticism is often shown to come from some point in the dark side. This is a rather curious problem with Star Wars as a whole: unless it is convenient for it to be the opposite, any and all criticism of the Jedi Order is shown to be a sign of the dark side. This is shown as a very binary set-up, with the Jedi being wholly white and most antagonists mostly black.

This dualism can be an interesting point to have in stories, such as the fall of the Jedi Covenant shown in the *Knights of the Old Republic* comic

# a mind (cont)

series, but this all too common showing forgets that even the Jedi have light-sided critics, the Jal Shey being one of them. And far too often, any Jedi who question the order are only given the "right" side of the Jedi or a perilous fall. This is a moral conundrum that calls into question the line of "Only Sith deal in absolutes" because they are often shown within narratives as the only two choices.

The fact is, the Jal Shey offer a very interesting third path. It is one that is clearly tied to the light side of the Force as shown through the *Campaign Guide*, and one that is highly intellectual and academic. Shouldn't they have had some of the same criticisms of the Jedi that has been brought up time and again in critical analysis of the Order and their actions? The Jal Shey would be a good way to address this, as well as serve as an option for those dedicated to the light side of the Force while being critical of the Order. There is no need for a blatant dark side fall for conflict within a story when a very esteemed order of Force Users dedicated to the lightside is also an available option for those critics. Even with an aforementioned slowness to recruit, the Jal Shey are a fascinating third option.

With the scuttling of the Expanded Universe in favor of a more "streamlined" approach to the Star Wars Universe, it seems like the Jal Shey may be scuttled entirely. This is a rather large shame, because the Jal Shey reveal within the Star Wars Universe a large unexplored part of it, a place where action archaeologists race Dark-Siders for ancient artifacts, a place where people just as skilled in The Force face off against an organization that forcibly conscripts children in the political and legal arena, and a place that would give a more nuanced and subtle approach to Star Wars. Subtlety may not be a thing that *Star Wars* is known for, but when done right, it can be done artisticly.

# J M Beal

## Science Fiction and Paranormal Author

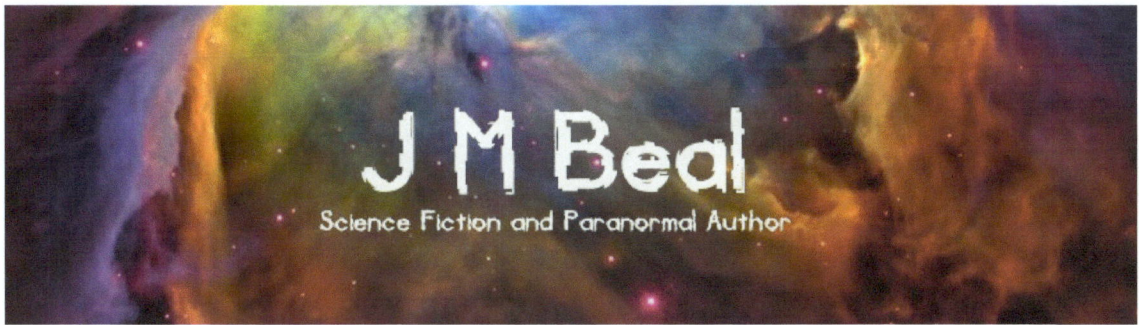

Rye Bartleby is a man who has made a career out of avoiding responsibility on two different colonial planets. When he runs into Addy Hallis on the street, he just can't make himself walk away, even after he's mistaken her for a saloon girl.

His life is getting ridiculously complicated, and everything is sideways, but he can't seem to make himself regret it.

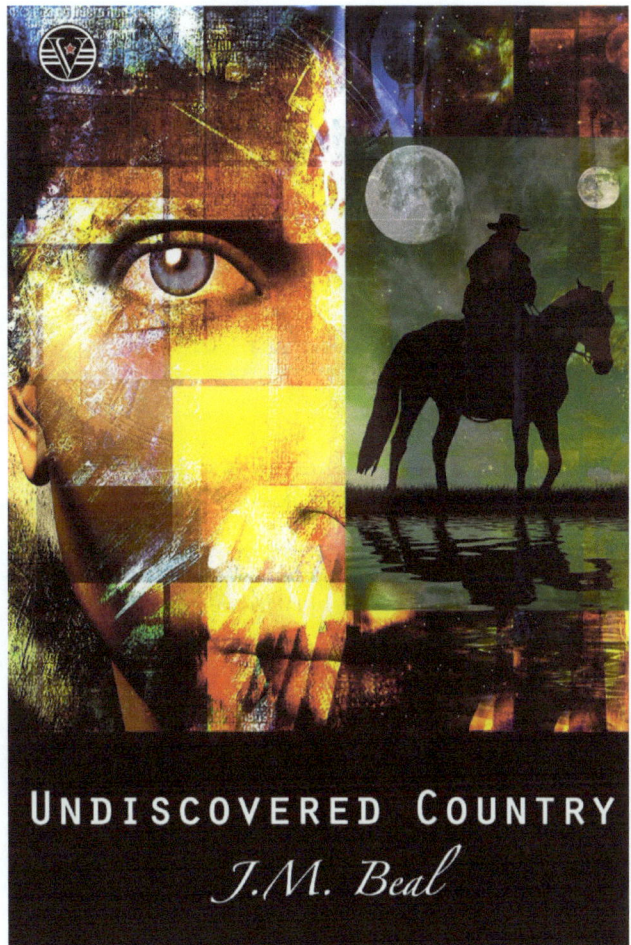

## UNDISCOVERED COUNTRY
### J.M. Beal

J M Beal's Undiscovered Country is available for purchase through Vagabondage Press and online retailers. For further information on upcoming publications, check out her website www. jmbeal.com!

THE FANDOM UNIVERSE

*Indelible Ink*

*A collection of essays about life in the Harry Potter fandom.*

**Coming November 2016!**

**goldenfleecepress.com/the-fandom-universe**

# In Defense of Jar Jar Binks
## Callie M. Ashton

Jar Jar Binks. That name alone is enough for most Star Wars fans to groan and roll their eyes. He is usually thought of as the worst mistake ever to grace the Star Wars Universe. Many fans think his role in the prequels was an unnecessary gimmick, while others claim that Lucas' attempt at comic relief came across as racist, equating it to a white actor parading around in black face, spewing racial stereotypes. He was stupid, clumsy, and voted in favor for Palpatine to take power over the Galactic Senate. Popular opinion states that he is a needless character that had no business being in the movies. Or was he?

Prior to the rise of the Galactic Empire, Naboo was having problems with the Trade Federation. After Queen Amidala came to power, she opened negotiations with the Trade Federation, who wanted to rule the planet and tried to bully Naboo into subjugation by blockading the planet. Amidala did not take kindly to the threats and asked the Jedi to intervene. The Jedi Counsel sent Jedi Master Qui-gon Jinn and his apprentice Obi-Wan Kenobi. The Trade Federation, under the leadership of Darth Plagueis and his apprentice Darth Sidious, was ordered to kill the Jedi, who escaped and ultimately ran into Jar Jar Binks. Because of the Gungan principle of life debt, Binks joined the Jedi, taking them to Otoh Gunga to meet the Gungan leader, Boss Nass. It was this meeting that changed the tide of the Battle of Naboo and altered the entire course of history. Binks became entangled in an ancient Jedi prophecy.

Enter the "Chosen One." The ancient Jedi prophecy foretold the coming of a person that would bring balance to the Force. The dark side of the Force is viewed as corrupt and destroyed the natural balance of life. One of the principle tenets of the Jedi Order is to restore that balance. The dark side was viewed as a cancer of the Living Force that was spread by the Sith. The prophecy stated that a being would be born in the greatest time of need and they would restore balance to the Force. That being was a product of the Force trying to counter balance the nefarious deeds of the Sith. Anakin Skywalker was born a vessel of

# In Defense (cont)

pure Living Force. He was the "Chosen One." Skywalker spent the first part of his life as a slave on Tatooine with his mother, Shmi. It was through a series of events—a few that may or may not have been altered by Master Jinn—that granted him his freedom, and he traveled to Naboo with the Jedi, Amidala, and Binks.

Once the group returned to Naboo, Binks led the way to the Gungan Sacred Place. It was during this time that Binks takes a bigger roll in the prophecy. After the Battle of Naboo, the Gungans and Naboo defeat the Trade Federation and make peace. The Gungans are now represented in the Galactic Senate with Binks as their representative. Unbeknownst to everyone, Darth Sidious and Darth Plagueis were in the midst of planning the biggest coup in the history of the Republic. The Sith Lords wanted to rule the galaxy. In order to do that, they needed control of the Senate.

So where does that put Jar Jar Binks? If you look at Palpatine's rise to power, you can see him ever so slightly plucking strings here and there, ever so quietly moving himself into power. I have no doubt that he used the Force to do so. He has Amidala call out the previous Chancellor because of the issues with the Trade Federation, the issues he, himself, caused. When Amidala returns to Naboo, he meets Binks and encourages the relationship with the Gungans. Why? Because he sees them as simple minded, easy to manipulate. If he has both the Naboo and Gungan representative on his side, they will be easier to manipulate—Binks more so than Amidala. Palpatine needed control, but he couldn't take it. He needed some one to encourage others to give it to him. That is all well and good, but what about the prophecy?

As previously stated, the Living Force created a perfect being to battle the horrors the Sith were doing, a balance. The Force is in everything—the Force *is* everything. In order to fulfill the prophecy, the Force created roles for people to play. Anakin Skywalker, the "chosen one." Obi-wan, the wise sage, the one who guides the chosen one down the path of this destiny. Padme

Amidala, the one that would cause the downfall of the chosen one. Luke Skywalker, the son that would ultimately save the father. And Jar Jar Binks, the one that had to start the rise of the Empire, the Judas Iscariot. Palpatine had to come into power. He killed his teacher, Darth Plagueis, so he did not have to share the power. He was ruthless and fully enveloped in the dark side of the Force, but he could not take it directly since that would alert the Jedi that he was a Sith. He needed the Galactic Senate to think they needed him, to think that he was the savior against the tyranny of the Trade Federation, to think he was the only option. He needed some one to convince the Senate. He knew that Amidala would not do that. He needed some one that was easily manipulated. He needed Jar Jar. He preyed upon the fears and innocence of what he considered a simple minded and backwards species. He had exploited the poor Gungan to set himself up in a position to take power. It is also quite possible that he manipulated Jar Jar's thoughts using something akin to the Jedi Mind Trick. He succeeded in his power grab and managed to turn Jar Jar Binks into the laughing stock of the Star Wars universe.

Unfortunately, he was setting up his own demise. As we know, Anakin was the one chosen to bring balance to the Force. Eventually, he did. He killed Darth Sidious to save his son. But what of Jar Jar? He continued to serve as a Senator throughout the Clone Wars, but learned to keep his mouth shut after the realizing his mistake of granting emergency power to the Chancellor which caused the bloodiest war in galactic history. He succeeded Amidala as a Senator in the Imperial Senate until he was replaced by Amidala's niece, Pooja Naberrie. He was considered an ally of the new Emperor, but faded away into obscurity.

So why was Jar Jar Binks so important? Because the Living Force made him so. The Living Force put him in the way of the Jedi on Naboo. By saving Qui-gon Jinn and Obi-wan Kenobi, he set into motion the events that would eventually save the galaxy and bring balance to the Force. Anakin needed the guidance of Kenobi and needed to suffer and feel the heartbreaking loss of losing his mother and wife in order for his redemption to take place. His salvation was his son. Without Palpatine becoming Emperor and having

# In Defense (cont)

everything at his disposal, Anakin would have died on Mustafar. Instead, he was saved and became Darth Vader, but at the moment of his death, he was the chosen one. He fulfilled the prophecy. Jar Jar Binks may have been a clumsy idiot. I mean, let's face it, he was, but he was chosen by the Living Force to play an important role in the prophecy. Somebody had to do it. Somebody had to betray the Senate. Somebody had to be paid the forty pieces of silver. Unfortunately for Jar Jar, that somebody was him and he will always be remembered as the bumbling idiot that voted in favor of a tyrant taking power instead of the hero he actually was.

# OPENING NIGHT
## JEFFERY COOK

*Star Wars* has had a large impact on my life from a very early age. When I was three, my parents went out to dinner for their first date night since my sister was born and brought me along. As they tell it, it was a very pleasant date. We ate Chinese food. I was well behaved and sociable.

Near the end of dinner, they decided that they were not ready for the night out to end. The Chinese restaurant was less than a block from the movie theater, so they started looking at what was playing. So, by random chance, luck, and good behavior, I was in the theater on opening night of Episode IV: *A New Hope*. I don't remember very much of it, but what I do remember is the Star Destroyer coming on screen for the first time. In fact, that moment is my earliest memory in life, and has been etched in my mind since.

Not long after, my scribbled pictures—which to that time had mostly been vaguely dinosaur-like things—started including space ships. Admittedly, the dinosaur-like things were usually beating up the evil space ships, but they found a place in my early imagination.

When *The Empire Strikes Back* came out, there was no accident or luck to it. I was in the audience opening night. This time I was old enough to understand everything that was happening, and I was firmly hooked. It wasn't long before kids in my class were playing Star Wars on the playground, and I managed to always be a Jedi. I was also reading by then, and whenever I could, I immersed myself in fantasy and science fiction. That wasn't all I read, but, partly inspired by my love of Star Wars—and the idea of the Jedi Knights—it became a favorite. As a six or seven year old, I began telling my mother about how I wanted to become an author when I grew up.

Obi-Wan Kenobi, and an ancient order of monks who wielded swords while everyone else had guns, and the elements of fantasy and swashbuckling against the outer space drama, inspired me far more than the other scifi of that day did. I liked *Star Trek*, and *Doctor Who*, and *Buck Rogers*, and *Star Blazers*, but I didn't love them. Where friends wanted spaceships, blasters, phasers, and so on, I wanted a sword—I'd found my fandom.

When *Return of the Jedi* came out, I was already a fan, and I do understand the people who say that Empire was objectively the best movie in the series. But *Return of the Jedi* is one of the defining moments of my childhood. When I think of the iconic scenes that inspire me in my own writing, it almost always goes back to the fight above the Sarlacc Pit and then the three-scenes-in-one finale, which not only had the Ewoks, it also had the epic lightsaber duel. I saw *Return of the Jed*i six times during opening week, including opening night. I don't regret a single one of those.

The later movies were not up to par, in my opinion. I'm not a fan of Jar Jar and I don't care for the midichlorians explanation for the Force. Lucas still does his best work writing roughs, and then letting other people direct. However, the battle vs. Maul is still the best choreographed lightsaber duel to date. Obi-Wan Kenobi remains my favorite character... and one of my favorites in all of fandom. There was enough to love to make it work for me. Episode II was better. Not great, but there was more swashbuckling, lightsaber duels, and Jedi badass-ery. I still didn't care for Anakin's acting, but Ewan McGregor made up for a lot, and got a lot of center-stage time. Episode III had steps forward and steps back—but it was still more of the universe I loved. And more importantly, it still had enough of the elements of the universe I fell in love with that I stuck with it.

Now, I make my living as a science fiction and fantasy author, as I dreamed of doing when I was six years old. I haven't written anything in regards to dinosaurs vs. space ships yet, but you never know... but I do have seven books published, covering steampunk, urban fantasy, scifi, and a couple YA variants of the above. I still feel I owe a lot of that imagination and inspiration to those early days, giving me something to embrace in the fandoms all my friends loved. When Sam Bowe in the *Dawn of Steam* books goes charging at gunmen, armed with nothing but a couple knives, or the characters find the Claiomh Solais (Sword of Light from Celtic mythology) as a central plot point in the *Fair Folk Chronicles*, there is definitely some of that old Jedi and lightsaber mystique pushing me, I think.

And now, we're about to get Episode VII. I'm not sure what to expect yet. I'm not sure if it will recapture some of the IV-VI mystique, or be more like I-III, with giant flaws, and hopefully at least enough Jedi for me to stay interested. But I am sure of one thing—just as I have been for every *Star Wars* movie to date, I'll be in the audience on opening night. I bought my ticket during the first hour they went on sale.

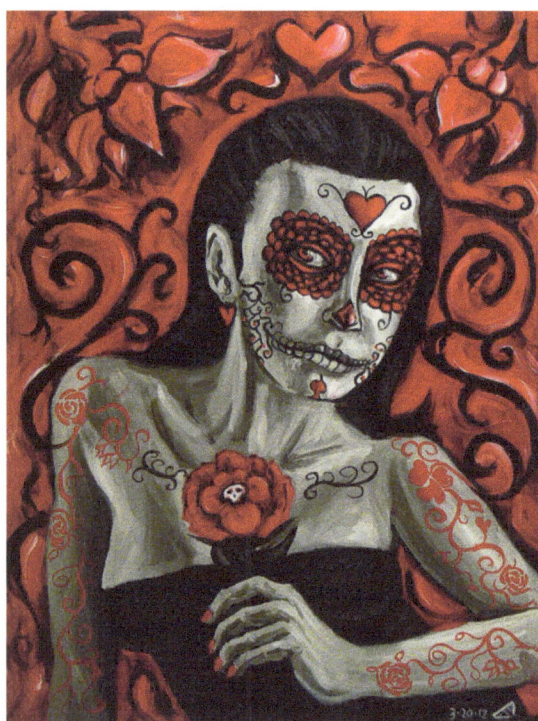
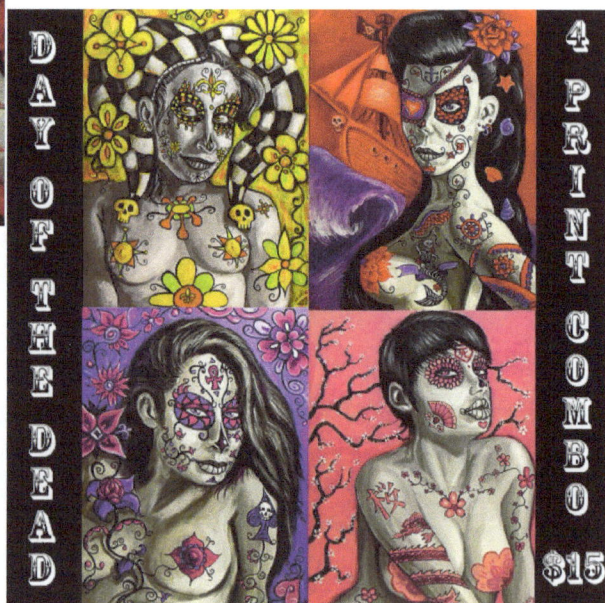
78

# On Science Fiction
## Julie Campbell Stoddard

Multiple times in May of 1977 I rode my bike five miles over busy highways and across an extension bridge that was only moderately safe in order to transport myself to a time long ago and far far away.

Conservatively, I saw *Star Wars:* Episode IV, *A New Hope* fifteen times. Not all of those trips required the scary bike ride. I talked my folks, my siblings, my friends and even my grandparents into going with me to see my new favorite movie. My grandmother was somewhat bewildered by the movie, but my grandfather, an armchair adventurer if there ever was one, loved it.

Sometime during the mid/late 1970's visual science fiction's aesthetics underwent a sea change. In reality, a number of TV series and movies displayed this change at more or less the same time, including the original *Battlestar Galactica*, and the *Buck Rogers* reboot. But from the point of view of a thirteen-year-old pop culture consumer, the vanguard of this visually used and dirty future was *Star Wars: A New Hope*.

The mid 1970's saw a cultural crosscurrent I wasn't aware of at the time, but that played out in all sorts of ways I see in retrospect. The end of the Vietnam War—and the visual images people saw intimately on television—and the 1976 Bicentennial with all of its bombast and nostalgia both had a real effect, in my opinion, on science fiction's visual aesthetic.

I was already a science fiction fan by 1977, even if Maine didn't have a lot of science fiction to pick from. I watched *Star Trek*. I loved the TV show *Space 1999*, with it's sealed habitat and runaway moon. The anime that I ran home from school to watch was *Space Battleship Yamamoto* (which I knew as *Star Blazers*). I'd seen *Logan's Run* and the post-apocalyptic *Planet of the Apes*. I sat through the dense and metaphoric *Space Odyssey 2001*.

I watched Creature Double Feature on Saturday afternoons, a TV movie slot comprised mostly of Japanese Kaiju movies, American horror movies and the stalwart,

# On Science Fiction (cont)

stern-jawed scientist heroes of the 1950's and their irradiated bug foes. These were occasionally leavened with an offering of a Hammer horror film or two, or the other thinly disguised horror films like *Island of Dr. Moreau*, *Westworld*, or *Soylent Green*. I wasn't and am not a big horror fan but beggar's wanting their science fiction can't afford to be choosy.

That was my philosophy all along, and I saw a lot of bad, dud movies that way.

*Star Wars* wasn't a dud. Neither, despite gossip to the contrary, was *Battlestar Galactica*, offered on the small screen here in the US (and in theatrical release outside the States) by Glen Larson's production company. Larson has also put together the *Buck Rogers* reboot.

All of a sudden, there was science fiction everywhere.

To me, before 1977, pure science fiction—in this case, speculation of what the future of mankind would look like—was defined by *Star Trek*, and by *Space 1999*. By the interior of Pertwee's Tardis in *Doctor Who*, and by the spaceship in *Space Odyssey 2001*. It was a very clean, white, uncluttered and nearly sterile future. The most exciting visual pops were the occasional moments of bright colors in the set dressing and the uniforms. Looking back, it all definitely had a mid-century modern look, with the wood tones exchanged for shades of white and gray.

Star Wars changed all that. The future that George Lucas envisioned was dirty, and dented. It was full of sand, worn out parts, and people who needed to be fixed. It looked real, just as much as it looked different.

The scorch marks on the BG's colonial Viper fighter ships were perhaps part of that larger sea change. The 1978 *Battlestar Galactica* came out after *Star Wars*, but they were filmed at the same time and on some of the same stages *Battlestar Galactica* had its theatrical movie release in Canada, Europe, and Japan at the same time as *A New Hope*.

In *Battlestar Galactica* the cleanest and most sterile environments belonged to the Cylons, pristine in their white, silver, and gold metallics. The humans were messy and their environments were a hodge-podge, often a tired one. Though BG's scripts didn't quite reach the promise of putting the human element first, visually, it was closer to Star Wars' dust and dents than to *Star Trek's* mid-century modern or to *Space Odyssey 2001's* pristine spaceship interiors.

On the other hand, *Buck Rogers*, written and run by the same people didn't follow that trend. It left me with the impression that the future, the good part anyway, looked pretty much like *Star Trek*, only without the pops of color. It was kind of boring. That may have been on purpose though, because as I remember it, Buck thought so too.

But from my point of view, as a thirteen-year-old pop culture consumer, Star Wars came first. Even in the 70's, full of self-indulgence, drugs and rock and roll, *Star Wars* bucked the rising trend of cynicism with its optimistic plot and characters. Luke and Han and Leia's universe may have been dented and dirty and worn out in places but it was also teetering on the brink of positive change.

To this day, my mental picture of the future includes the wear and tear of humanity on the world around us, but it also includes a certain level of inner optimism. We are "big damn heroes"[1] if we need to be—even if our ships need some "pocking with a wrench"[2] to keep them going. We can ground our visions of the future in the grit of reality even while we promise ourselves to build a better one.

In waves, the dark times come and go. We greet them with intestinal fortitude and heart. These are the stories that we tell ourselves. We frame them in visual ways, as well as in words. They define our future for us. They are good stories with spine, belief and a passion to make things better for us all; *Star Wars: A New Hope* still exemplifies the best part of that.

1. This phrase is from Joss Whedon's TV series *Firefly*

2.This phrase is from a series of military SF books by John Ringo, "The March to..." books.

It's not TV or a movie but I think the point still stands and expands (so to speak) to other mediums – but that's a whole other essay.

# Craftus Interuptus
# or Hot Glue Is Not The Force
## Kate Ressman

I grew up as a *Star Wars* fan—Jawa tee-shirt as a kid, stuffed Ewoks, extended universe books. Therefore, I was excited for Episode I. Not sleep-out-in-the-rain excited, but ready to see it opening weekend. I knew nothing would compare to the original movies for me, but I was optimistic. I knew nothing would meet the hype and excitement, the stories in my brain from the books and the net, but I was bouncy and ready to drag my friend with me.
It was... well, at least it level set my expectations for Episode II. But there was still a buzz from the movie and a joy to be back in the universe. I fell head-first into the internet fandom. And I wasn't alone.

For the first time I wanted to be a Jedi, not a smuggler. And I still wasn't alone. Obi-Wan and Qui-Gon swiftly won me over.

My best friend was just as enthusiastic. More maybe. But the excitement between us echoed and grew until we commenced a weekend of Star Wars crafting. We were going to be Jedi by Halloween or die trying. (This was before I would have ever thought of going to a con. Maybe before I even really acknowledged that they existed.) We haunted the craft and sewing center.

Three stores later, we got brown fabric for cloaks and leading to make them drape. Beige cotton came home for shirts and pants. We even found brown pleather for holsters and belts. But—and I should have seen the problem, but no, I was too confident—there were no "space wizard" costume patterns then. There was no craft marketing for *Star Wars*. So, we brought a standard Vogue pattern that looked good for the shirt and a monk's costume to modify for the cloak.

Savvy sewers will have caught my fatal errors: I picked up a Vogue pattern (so. many. pieces.) and I was prepared to modify my second pattern.

During this jaunt to the crafting meccas, we decided that we needed communicators, food capsules, and—of course— lightsabers. Research time! The costumes were set aside for a research bender: pictures, behind-the-scenes interviews with prop people, a rewatching of the movie or two. Then, off to the hardware store for steel pipes, fuses, pipe covers, and a grinding wheel; the stationary shop for roller ball pens who's brand escapes me; the craft store for spray paint and blue tape. And no alcohol to blame any of this on. At the time I didn't drink. I would come to regret that soon.

So we started on the lightsabers while we had the house to ourselves and access to the grinder. I'm sensing a few raised brows asking me why we needed to use a grinder for a Halloween prop. Because it needs to be right, okay?

So as the light faded from the sky, showers of sparks that shimmered like fireworks poured out of the garage door. This also meant that sparks fell on my hands and the metal was at lava temperature when the final kerchunk meant we'd made it through.

Did I mention this was our first metal grinding experience? Hey! I still have all my fingers and both eyes.

The lightsabers shaped up well, with spigot fittings and spray painted fuses. But. Well. We didn't have super-glue. So, yeah, we put them aside.

Time to break out the shirt pattern. A shirt should be about ten pieces. Not hard right? [Insert wild laughter here] No. See, we bought a Vogue pattern. I think the final count was 1,400 pieces. Something like that. We overcame for awhile.

The shirt and pattern are still haunting the basement. Maybe I should try again now that I'm older, more experienced, saner. One of the three at least.

Luckily, the two bolts of expensive, drive-to-three-stores brown fabric haven't been cut. They're just glowering at me from the project bag. It's not that I care any less for Star Wars, it's just that I want those cloaks to be perfect. I want the sleeves long enough to hide my hands and the folds to flow properly when I walk. I don't want a brown bathrobe.

On to the one piece that got finished, the communicator. I can't claim much on this one though. I think I made the holster for it. That used a sewing

# craftus Interuptus (cont)

machine, not a hot glue gun, so I'm pretty safe with that assertion. I don't think my bestie will mind me claiming this one. I mean, I probably sprayed it silver right? (Oh yeah, that is a lady's razor under that paint. Just like the original from the movie. PERFECT remember?)

Maybe it's all for the best that the Disney marketing mavens are all over the merchandising for the new movie. I can easily get all the make-believe props I want.

But, well, I won't love them as much as a spray painted razor and a half-done lightsaber. Even if I do have burn scars from the sparks.

So if you'll excuse me, there's a new movie, see, and I bet that I can get that cloak done in time...

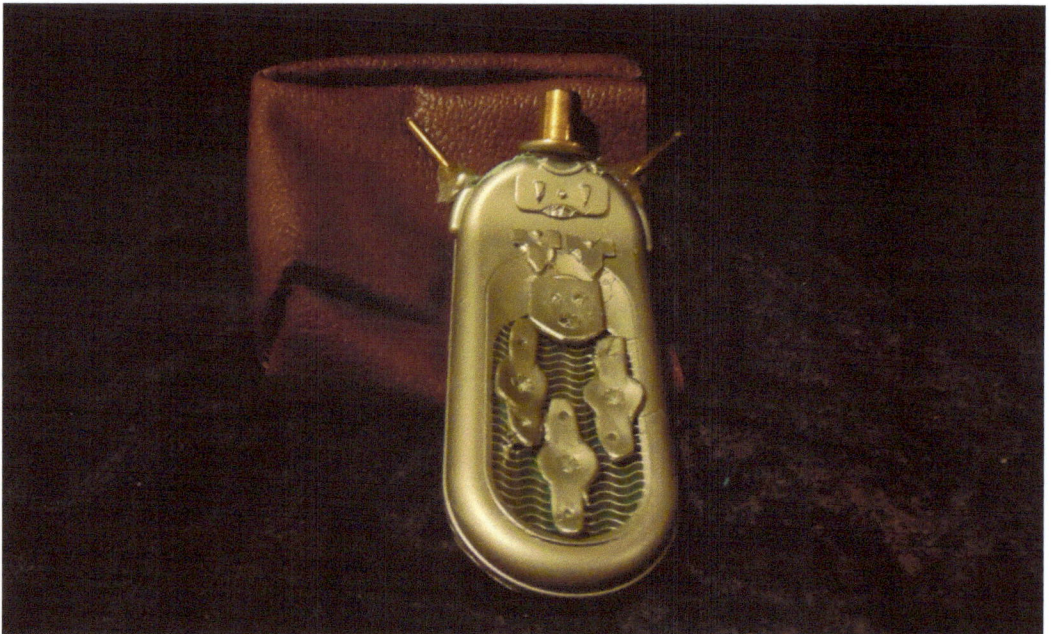

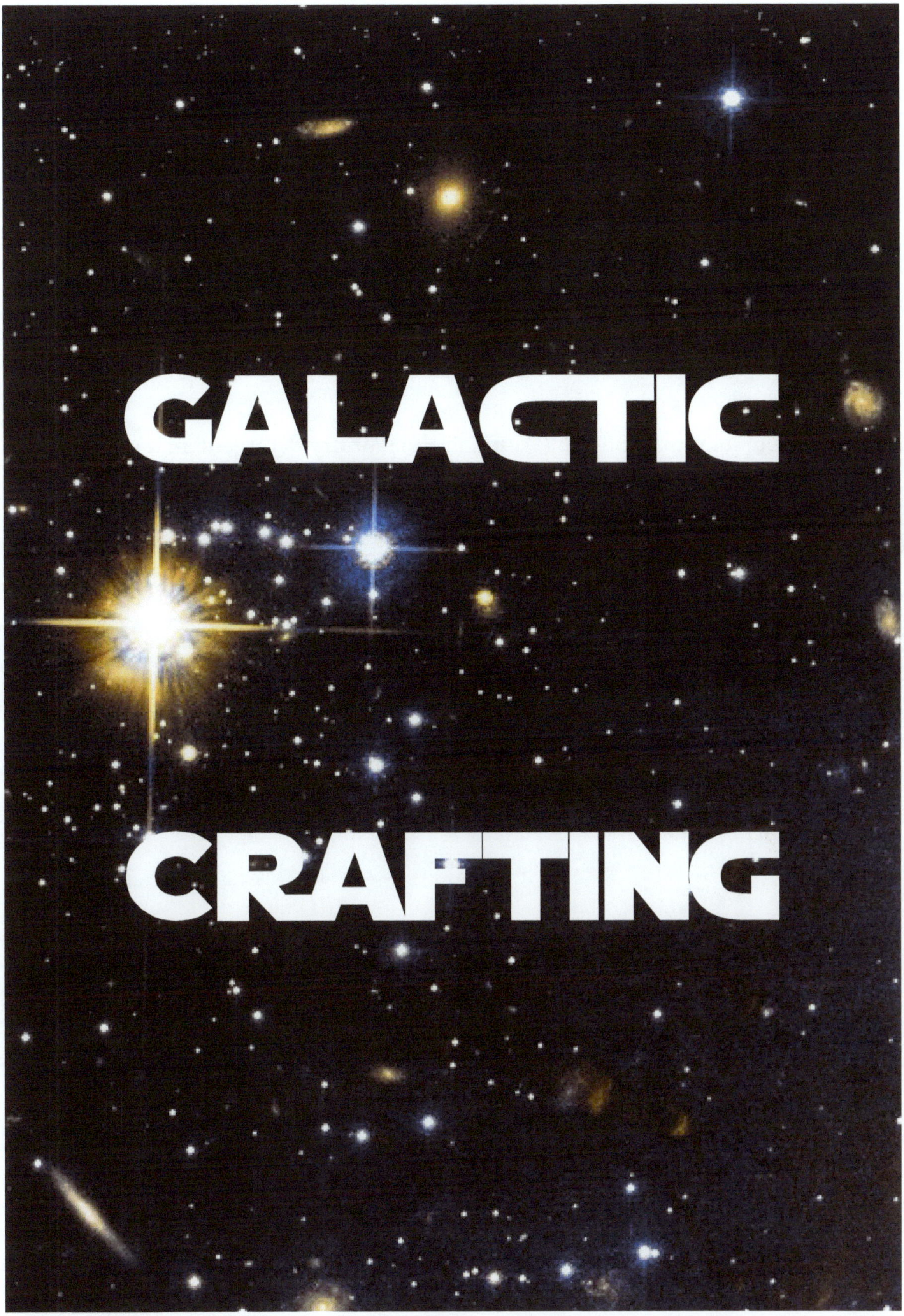
GALACTIC
CRAFTING

# GALAXY SLIME

When you are a kid, crafting is always fun. Making messes even more so. Galaxy Slime is the best of both worlds. It is fun to make, easy to clean up afterwards, and provides hours of entertainment.

Ingredients:

Clear Elmer's Glue

1/2 Cup of Liquid Starch (Found in the laundry detergent aisle)

Various Colors of Glitter

Various Colors of Food Coloring

Various Colors Acrylic Paint (Optional)

Gloves and wooden crafting stick (for mixing)

Bowl(s)

*You can also use clear glitter glue. It comes in a variety of colors.

<u>Step One</u>:  Mix the glue, coloring, and glitter in a bowl. It is best to use a wooden crafting stick.

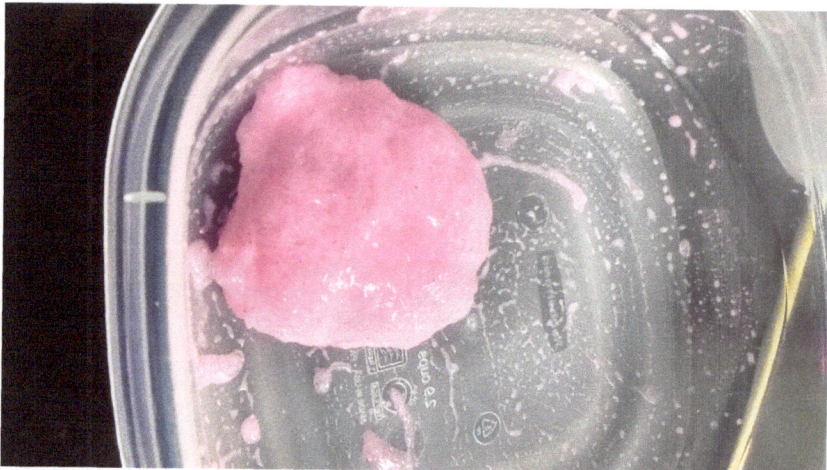

**Step Two:** It is best to use your hands during this step. Add starch and mix well. Check the consistancy. If it is too thin or too sticky, you will need to add more starch. Add a little at a time, no more than 1 teaspoon, until the texture feels like slime. You can also add acrylic paint during this step to add more color.

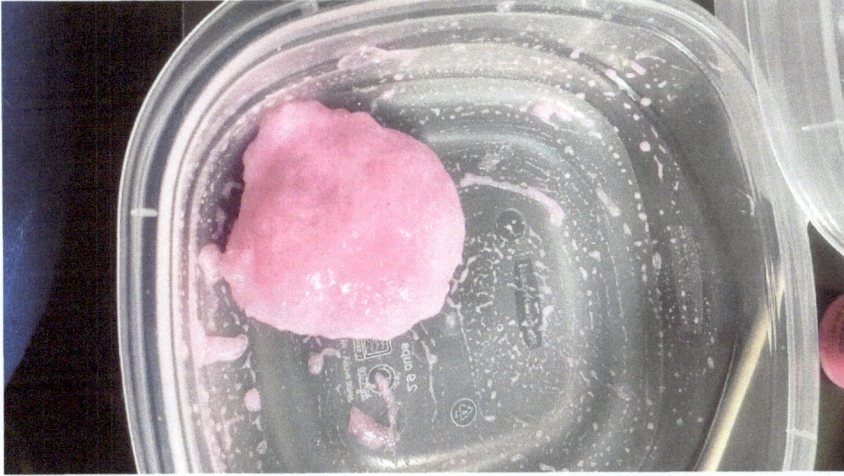

**Step Three:** Repeat the process with different colors. Adding small star confetti adds a fun element to the slime. You can also mix the different colors together to make a really cool galaxy effect.

# NEBULA JARS

Nebula Jars are another fun craft to do. They make great girfts and it is fun coming up with different designs. They take only a few ingredients and are very quick to do. Plus, they just look really cool.

### Ingredients
Glass Jar With A Lid (any size)
Glitter/Confetti
Water
Food Coloring of Various Colors
Cotton Balls
Long Wooden Craft Stick for Mixing
Mixing Bowls

**Step One**: Prepare your water with the food coloring of your choice. The amount of water depends on how large your jar is. It is best to use various shades of reds, blues, and purples.

**Step Two**: Line the bottom of your jar with cotton balls. Again, the amount depends on the size of your jar, but you need enough to cover the bottom of the jar.

**Step Three**: Pour the first color into your jar. There should be enough to soak all the cotton with a little bit left over.

**Step Four:** Add your glitter and use your stick to poke the cotton on the sides to spread the glitter down the sides.

**Step Five:** Repeat the steps with all of your colors.

Make sure your lid is properly sealed. You can glue the lids if need be. Also, DO NOT SHAKE! It will mix all of the colors together and you will end up with sludge. You can use large jars or bottles to use as a decoration or you can use tiny jars for jewelry, which are pictured below.

The possiblilities are endless.

*Photo by Flying Snails Treasures. Used with permission.*

# Galaxy Dough

Who doesn't like Play-Doh? Most of us spent out young lives squishing the stuff between out fingers. What could make it better? Glitter. Lots and lots of glitter. The following recipe is rather simple and kids will love making their own dough.

Ingredients
1 Cup of Water
1/2 Cup of Salt
2 Teaspoon of Cream of Tartar
2 Tablespoons of Vegetable Oil
1 Cup of Flour (white)
Food Coloring

**Step One:** Combine water and food coloring of your choice. Black makes a really cool "spacy" color, but you can use the color of your choice.

**Step Two:** Add water, salt, and cream of tartar in a medium sauce pan. Cook on low heat and stir with a wooden spoon

**Step Three:** Stir in flour and keep stiring until it looks dry. It will pull away from the sides of the sauce pan. Remove from heat. Pinch between fingers to test consistancy. When it is not sticky, it is ready.

**Step Four:** Dump the dough on the counter and let cool for 10 minutes then knead the dough as your would bread. Be careful, it will be warm!

<u>**Step Five**</u>: Add your mix-ins and have fun! You can increase the recipe and make all sorts of colors. Mixing dark blues, purples, and black makes a really cool galaxy effect.

Editor's Note: I decided to go with a lighter blue instead of a black and the glitter colors did not come out as well as I hoped. I think the black food color and maybe larger glitter would work better. I used a variety of colors of glitter, but gold and orange worked better with my color of dough. I still love my galaxy dough. It sits on my desk and serves as a stress ball.

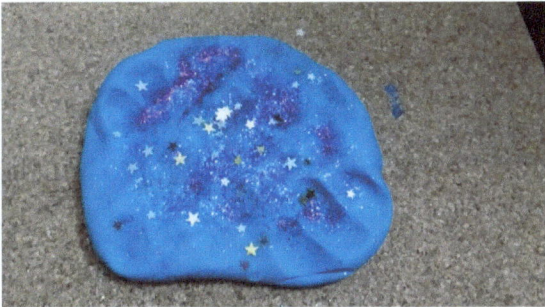

# Space Painting

You gotta admit it, nebulae are breathtakingly beautiful. The way the dust and ionized glasses swirl around reminds me of colorful clouds. In fact, the word "nebula" comes from the Latin word for "cloud". Most nebulae are emourmous, hundreds of light years in diameter. Some create stars while others are the remains of supernovas. Either way, they are beautiful. Below are instructions on how to paint a nebula. It is a fun craft to do with children or on your own. Be warned though, it get a bit messy. Children should be supervised by an adult.

Supplies:
Acetate (I used self-laminating sheets)
Cotton Balls or Sponge Brushes
Acrylic Paint in Various Colors
Glitter of Various Colors

Step One: Cut your acetate to desire size. I used 4 by 6 self-lamnating sheets.

Step Two: Starting with a drop or two of the color of you choice, spread the paint using a cotton ball by dabbing the paint.

**Step Three**: Continue this method with the rest of your colors until you are happy with it. Make sure you use one cotton ball per color. If not, you could end up mixing colors you don't want mixed. And remember-- less is more. Start with small amounts of paint. You can always add more.

# Space Painting (cont)

**Step Four:** (Optional) Once you are finished with your paint, you can add glitter to give your painting a little extra shiny. You need to make sure to do this when the paint is still wet so the glitter properly sticks.

That is it! Let the painting dry and hang it up somewhere.

# Welcome to the Fandom Universe

# Golden Fleece Press

What makes a fan? What's more important, canon or interpretation? How many collectables does it take to fill your basement?

These are important, burning questions. They're questions we want you, the fan, to help us answer. And admit it, you've been studying your entire life to answer them.

This anthology has focused on Star Wars. We've covered everything from video games, to Jar Jar. We've talked about the serious and the frivolous. Have we covered it all? Not even close. But the printing costs on 800 pages of fan critique is exactly as prohibitive a you'd think it is, and then we'd have to ask the Empire to subsidize the shipping, and it's all downhill from there.

All the people involved in this anthology are fans, just like we hope the people enjoying it are.

So what does that mean for you?

"We want you!" she bellows in her best, world war two era, Uncle Sam voice.

We've got plans, friend. Maybe, on the earlier pages you saw an ad for *Indelible Ink*, coming in November 2016. That's our next plan. Everyone has a Potterverse story, right? We're banking on it.

After that, the worlds are our oyster. *Star Trek*. *Doctor Who*. Sherlock Holmes. Do you have an affinity for Joss Whedon? Are you a Marvelite or a DC'er? The list could go on for ages.

We suspect it'll keep getting longer as we go. That's fine, we'll be here as long as you are.

And hey, find us on social media and tell us which project you think we should do after *Indelible Ink*. We're big fans of audience participation.

www.ingramcontent.com/pod-product-compliance
Lightning Source LLC
Chambersburg PA
CBHW061046090426
42740CB00002B/58